Chapters in a Spiritual Life

Chapters in a Spiritual Life

Ralph A. Steadman

Stellium Ltd

Published in 2020 by Stellium Flame,
an imprint of Stellium Ltd
Plymouth, Devon UK
Tel: +44 (0)1752 367 300   Fax: +44 (0)1752 350 453

Copyright © 2020 Ralph A. Steadman
Ralph A.Steadman has asserted his moral right
to be identified as the author of this work
in accordance with sections 77 & 78 of
The Copyright, Designs and Patents Act 1988

British Library Cataloguing in Publication Data:
A catalogue record for this book is available
from The British Library

Cover design and illustrations copyright © 2020
Jan Budkowski, Pixabay
ISBN: 978-1-912358-06-9

About the Author

After getting a law degree in 1954, Ralph Steadman spent nine years in the Army, mostly in Army Education. Returning to civilian life in 1963, he worked for IBM for a time, before using his computer knowledge to work in companies pioneering computerised insurance, and then computerised management of large construction projects.

In 1967, Ralph became a Training Officer in the newly formed Road Transport Industry Training Board, from which – many years later – he was 'head-hunted' to be Education and Training Manager of a large, multi-branch organisation in the retail Motor Trade. He ended his working life doing what he most loved - teaching – before retiring in 1999.

Ralph now lives in Torquay with his second wife, Sybil – a gifted clairvoyant healer – and is actively involved in local Spiritualism. He has written several books and still lectures at Spiritualist conferences. Ralph lists among his other interests, music, computers and learning languages (of which he has studied eleven, at one time or another.)

Ralph says of himself, 'For the last fifty years I have been interested in psychic phenomena in general and spiritual philosophy in particular. Over the last few years, this has expanded into the study of Metaphysics – what lies beyond Science and also Religion – which I believe is the area that contains the answers to all possible questions about the ultimate reality of life.'

Dedication

I dedicate this book to Kim, a very dear friend, gifted healer and platform medium, who sits with us during our regular home circles. One week she was told by her inspirers that I had to write a book and she told me what it had to be about. Thereafter, she nagged me every session to get me to start writing – until I eventually gave in.

Contents

Preface

I have now written three spiritual books, the first, entitled "A New Understanding of Life", was published on the internet in 2010. It was a channelled book, and it introduced me to Metaphysics – or that which is beyond Science and also beyond Religion, but strangely enough, this is also the area where Science and Religion meet and mutually support each other. The second, entitled "A Practical Spiritual Primer", was published in spring 2017, and was a very full exposition of spiritual philosophy, including a study course as an appendix. At the end of 2017, I wrote "Spiritualism under the Microscope", as a general introduction to Spiritualism for non-Spiritualists, giving factual answers to seventy questions which newcomers might ask about it.

This present book doesn't add any additional information to what is given in "The Primer", which is quite a comprehensive book, and in fact it duplicates several of the stories told there, but it outlines my own life story, and shows how I came to the level of spiritual knowledge that I have to date. (I am still learning, of course, even at my advanced age. In fact, I quote an event which gave me further enlightenment only a couple of months ago.) It particularly explains the answer to the age-old question of which is the truth: Freewill or Predestination, and it will show how that puzzle worked out in my own life.

So which of my books would I recommend to you, dear potential reader? Well, if you are completely new to Spiritualism, the "Microscope" book is the best one to start you off. If you are an experienced Spiritualist, the "The Primer" will give you a lot of in-depth knowledge. If you are ready to go into some very deep philosophical (and practical) ideas, then the internet book is best, although it is far more difficult to read. (One of the drawbacks is that it is printed in tiny 10-point typeface.)

However, should you wish to explore it, go to my website, www.wolfeagle.co.uk – for a link.

So where does this present book stand in the series? It is really for those who wish to go a little further than just basic facts about Spiritualism but aren't yet ready to get really into the depth of philosophy which "The Primer" contains. For those who have read "The Primer" and enjoyed it – and possibly enjoyed some of my lectures at one time or another – this book may well serve to help you to understand me, and "where I am coming from" – my own spiritual journey. It has been quite an eventful journey to date, and hopefully the book will provide some interesting facts about life pre-war and immediately post-war for those of you who are not yet sixty years of age.

One of the surprising things about the book is that it shows how I was introduced to the subject of Astrology – which to some, is a most un-spiritual study – and how I have used it as part of my spiritual counselling work.

For those of you who buy this book, I hope that you have as much pleasure in reading it as I have had in writing it, and of recalling my long spiritual journey back to my first adult reading from a Spiritualist medium, 63 years ago.

Introduction

Is Spiritualism a religion or not? As far as I am concerned, it is not. You can be a Spiritualist and also a Christian, following the Greater World pattern, or not a Christian, following the SNU pattern. Some non-Spiritualist Christians are also attracted by Spiritualist beliefs, particularly when grieving deeply for the loss of a loved one. In fact, in our local congregation we have a devout Catholic who, two months after the passing of her husband, happened to visit my wife and me when a medium friend was with us. Within the first ten minutes our friend gave her impromptu messages from her two late husbands and her long-lost father. She was intrigued enough to visit our Centre for the next of our weekly evenings of clairvoyance, and for the next eight weeks received messages through eight different mediums confirming what she had been told. She is now a valued member of our congregation.

It is also possible for members of other religions to be interested in Spiritualism. For instance, two devout Muslims are regulars at both our Centre and a local Spiritualist church. When I spoke to the man, a very learned gentleman, and expressed my surprise that he attended Spiritualist meetings, he told me that basically, stripped of all extremist dogma, there were a lot of similarities between Islam and Spiritualism.

Now it is not possible to be a member of two religions at the same time. It would be as stupid to say that someone is a Christian Muslim as to say that he is a Hindu Jew. So Spiritualism cannot be a religion; but if it isn't a religion, then what is it?

To me, it is a way of life. It provides a basic belief system which can help us to understand and get through our life in a satisfactory way and accept what happens in that life, good or bad, in a philosophical manner, living one day at a time. It provides encouragement in times of stress and comfort in times of despair. In addition, it creates a framework which sets this present life in the greater framework of the life of the Universe itself. Finally, it shows us that our life is bound by the same law as that of the Universe, the immutable law of Cause and Effect.

Thinking about this, I was led to consider some of the events in my own life, and to explore what led me to my original acceptance of Spiritualist beliefs, and then – once I had become a Spiritualist – what things happened which either added to my existing knowledge, or led me into other avenues of research. My journey has been a long one – I am now more than half-way through my eighties – and contained many changes of fortune, some of which I saw at the time as being not to my advantage. However, with the wisdom of hindsight, I can now see that everything formed part of a pattern of progress, not always *material* progress but certainly *spiritual* progress. Very often – I might almost say *usually* – what appeared to be a disaster at the time turned out to be a blessing in disguise?

The most extreme example of this was in 1993, when I was 59 years of age, and I lost my beloved wife after 38 years. (I didn't *lose* her, of course, she just died. I will never lose her: she is only ever a thought away from me.)

However, at the time this represented complete catastrophe in my life. It was the ending of all our hopes and dreams, and for a long time it seemed like the ending of my own life, with nothing more to look forward to or hope for.

However, today I can look back on the 26 years since her passing and see that *spiritually* it was an actual blessing. In case this sounds disrespectful to her memory, let me say that in the last twenty years I have progressed more spiritually than I ever did in the previous 65, and none of this could have happened in the environment that I was then in.

There are, of course, dangers in going back over the past: if we are honest, there are things which happened in our life, things that we did or didn't do, of which we are deeply ashamed. Opening up the past may prove to be a real "Pandora's box", bringing to light things which we thought had been hidden away for ever.

Introduction

Some can never be disclosed, as doing so would adversely affect people who are still living. Others, however, can be safely unearthed, acknowledged, and finally accepted as lessons making up the rich tapestry of life itself. If we can realise that everything which has happened in our life, "good" or "bad", has brought us to where we are today, with the knowledge and wisdom which we now have, then we have made a massive step towards our own enlightenment.

One such incident in my own life, apparently trivial, but which affected me for many years, was during my early marriage. We had gone to a local cinema where a new "blockbuster" children's film was being shown for the first time. We arrived early, before the doors opened, and there was a small queue, at the front of which was a boy about ten years old. When the doors opened, he was first at the pay-desk, and offered his money, for a child's ticket. However, he was told that as it was a special performance, there were no reduced prices, so he would have to pay the full adult price of 2s 6d (12.5 pence in modern money) – which he didn't have. He began to cry bitterly, and for a couple of minutes everyone stood uncomfortably and wondered what would happen. I was impressed to pay for his ticket – but I didn't.

That simple incident seared itself into my memory, and I have always bitterly regretted my inaction. I don't know why I didn't do anything: the sum involved – although worth a lot more than it would be today – was trivial to me at the time, and it would have been so easy to step in and help, but I didn't, and the sight of that lad walking away crying still remains with me to this day, some sixty years later. In fact, as I write these lines now the memory still brings tears to my eyes.

However, in a small way that incident was the first in a series which has brought me to the realisation that helping others doesn't mean that we have to make grand gestures, or do anything spectacular at all. Helping others can be done in ways which seem completely trivial to us, but which mean a great deal to the other person.

Contrary to what most people think, giving money to someone is not necessarily the best way to help them, (certainly if they are drug addicts or alcoholics). Even a smile or a kindly word can mean a lot to someone who is lonely or depressed. I am reminded of the story of a man walking along a beach after a storm at sea, when the beach was littered with starfish which had been washed up. He was throwing some back into the sea when another man came up and said, "Why are you doing that? There are so many that you can't possibly make a difference by throwing a few back." The man picked up another, threw it back, and replied, "I made a difference to *that* one."

So that is what this book will be about, a series of reflections on the events in my own life, and how those events taught me lessons and eventually gave me the experiences which have formed my overall philosophy of life. I do not suggest that all of the conclusions which I have reached will be acceptable to everyone – in fact, I know that they won't – but hopefully enough of them will resonate with you, dear reader, to make it worthwhile for you to read this book.

I still haven't finished my quest for knowledge, as now I have progressed into studying Metaphysics, which is the area beyond Religion and also beyond Science, but more about that later.

Chapter One: Early Days

I suppose that my introduction to spirituality started when I was very young. My mother was a very devout Christian, from a strict Church of England family, so I was destined to be indoctrinated into religion at a very early age. I don't know how old I was when I started going to church with her, when she attended Evensong at the local church every Sunday, but I couldn't have been more than 5 years old. (My father, although baptised into the Church of England, very rarely attended church.)

That evening service didn't teach me anything at all about *spirituality*, but it taught me a lot about *formality*. All the members of the regular congregation had their own preferred seats, and woe betide anyone who sat in the wrong seat by mistake. (For them the command of the Master Jesus to love one another had a rider added to it; unless he is sitting in your seat at church.) Everyone was formally dressed of course, and an air of solemnity hung round the whole church like a pall. People acknowledged each other formally, without obvious warmth. Anything approaching displays of pleasure at meeting others was frowned on, and smiles or – God forbid – laughter would have been severely censured as immodest conduct. All in all, it was a very dreary and enervating experience, which to a small child was a feat of endurance.

About two years later, my mother had me enrolled in the choir, and church life became more interesting. I had a good treble voice, and learnt to sight-read fairly quickly. It was made easier by the fact that the trebles sang only the top notes of chords – the main tune of the hymns, most of which I knew already – so in those days, I had no need of learning the intricacies of harmony. However, what was completely new to me was the music of the morning services, which were in a form (full Choral Eucharist) almost unheard of in modern churches.

I enjoyed my years in the choir, and that early grounding, under the tuition of a very strict choirmaster called Mr Pedley, started my lifelong love of music, which has given me a great deal of pleasure over the years.

So what spiritual value did I get out of my years of attending church? Well not a lot from the non-musical side. I always thought the prayers very depressing. (I remember particularly the vicar, Oswald Nield – an old man long past his sell-by date – droning things like "Have mercy on us poor, miserable sinners", and "We are not so much worthy as to gather up the crumbs under thy table", which is hardly likely to inspire or uplift anyone, let alone a young boy.) As for the sermons, most of what was said went over my head, so we choirboys used to be more interested in whispering to each other during them, much to the wrath of the choir-men sitting behind us.

However, the music was a totally different kettle of fish entirely. For those who have never experienced it, there is nothing more uplifting than to be a member of a choir, (in those days, of course, it was exclusively a male-voice choir,) all singing in perfect harmony. Today you can get some idea of the power of music to uplift spiritually by listening to recordings of choirs, particularly mixed-voice choirs like the Mormon Tabernacle choir singing "the Battle Hymn of the Republic"; but nothing compares with the amazing experience of being *part* of a choir, and "in the middle of" the music which is being produced.

Many years later, as an adult in the Army, I experienced this in a completely unique way. I was in the Army, with NATO in France, and one Christmas someone had the bright idea of having an international carol service in the local church. Each country represented (there were about eight or ten nations there in the base) produced a choir, which gave a rendering of one carol which typified Christmas in that country, so all were different. However, for the grand finale, all choirs sang the one carol which is known and loved by Christian communities all over the world – "Silent Night."

Early Days

It was a very memorable service, a real feast of music, but the culmination, with everyone singing the carol in their own language, but in perfect musical harmony, was an experience which was beyond description, and everyone in the church was greatly moved – some to tears.

However, there is an even greater effect which my experience of singing in a choir had on me, and that is that in a wider context I realise the pleasure which can be experienced by being part of a team, all working towards a common goal. Just as in a choir, where all the members are singing different parts which blend in to make a completely harmonious sound, so when we work in a team we don't need to all do the same thing – we do our part, which blends in with what others are doing in order to get the job done.

This is particularly appropriate in a Spiritualist environment, of course. How many people, watching a gifted medium perform, say "I wish that I could do that", and belittle themselves because they can't? Each of us has a spiritual gift – some more than one; but not being able to do one thing doesn't mean that people are failures: it just means that they are not thinking in a wider context, about what gift(s) *they* might have which are not being used at the time.

Let me give a simple example of how a hidden spiritual gift might be used to great advantage. When people go into a new environment, such as going to a church or centre for the first time, there is always a slight apprehension about whether or not they will feel comfortable there, and be accepted. So many people have come away from such a first experience saying, "No-one spoke to me, and I didn't feel welcome there at all" – and that was the last time they went there.

However, there are a lot of lovely people who go to services and demonstrations who are very sociable and friendly who could well act as "hostesses" to talk to newcomers. (I apologise for being "sexist" there, but I have always found that there are far more women than men who go to Spiritualist services/ demonstrations.) It wouldn't take a lot of effort on their part: just walking up to somebody and saying, "Is this your first time here"? (They will already know that it is.) "Did you find it interesting?" "What inspired you to come?" Simple questions like that will "break the ice" and start the people talking, which will immediately make them feel good because someone has actually *noticed* them.

There are some places which have a very welcoming atmosphere. In my own experience, these tend to be usually centres rather than churches, although there are some very notable exceptions; but I wonder how many places have an actual organisation which *deliberately* provides a welcoming service to newcomers. In fact, are there any at all? If not, perhaps it is time that someone thought seriously about setting one up – it would certainly give an outlet for those social people who bewail their own lack of a spiritual gift.

Back to the subject of working together as a team, in the Centre where I attend clairvoyant demonstrations weekly, there is no committee. There is one lady who is in overall charge of policy and organisation, but there are a lot of people "doing their own thing" as well, running the raffle, running the canteen, giving healing, doing one-to-one mini-readings (clairvoyance, Tarot, Psychometry, Harmony Board), practitioners in reflexology and foot-reading, spiritual and bereavement counselling and spiritual philosophy. No-one interferes with anyone else's work, and there is never any need for joint discussions. If there is anything proposed which could affect the overall running of the Centre, the "Boss" will consult people individually but she will make the final decision, and no-one will object.

Here, I have to admit that I am not a fan of committees, for several reasons. It has been my experience that many people get themselves voted onto committees purely to find out what is going on behind the scenes. They are very vocal in proclaiming their own ideas as to what *should* be done, but when it comes to the question of actually *doing* something to make it happen, they are curiously lacking in volunteering. So that although there may be eight – or even ten – on a committee, there are usually only two or three who actually *do* the work.

Also, I have seen too many cases where "cliques" form in committees, and in extreme cases one clique will conspire against members of another in order to get rid of them, and impose their own ideas for the running of the organisation.

Early Days

Finally, there are many people who get onto committees purely as a boost to their own self-esteem, so that they can impress others with their own importance.

That is why, when Sybil and I took over the running of a local evening of clairvoyance, we didn't have a committee, and when that place eventually evolved into Infinity Clairvoyance, the foremost centre of Spiritualism in Torbay, that policy has been continued today in the present running of the centre.

Going back to my early days, although my time in the choir, which lasted about ten years, was very enjoyable and gave me a lifelong interest in music, there was another aspect of my early religious experience which was to prove far more important, not to mention character-forming, and that was the Sunday School, which I attended from the age of seven until I went to University at the age of seventeen.

I adored going to Sunday school. It was quite a big school, with thirty or more pupils split up into classes by age, and four or five teachers. At the start of each year, each pupil was given a small stamp book, and a stamp for attendance was given each week to be stuck in the book. Then at the end of each school year there was a prize-giving, and of course those who had the most stamps in their book got the best prizes. I was always in the top section of prizes, as nothing – except extreme illnesses, which were fortunately very few – would keep me away from attending.

I had a vivid imagination, and loved the Bible stories which we were told weekly. To me they weren't just stories; I got so immersed in them that it felt almost as though I was there at the time, experiencing what the Biblical characters were experiencing. Also, being blessed with a high intelligence, I could remember each story long after it had been told, a gift which soon came to the notice of my current teachers, so that I became quite a 'star pupil". Much later, when I was about fifteen, this led to me being appointed a teacher myself, a rare honour, as most of the teachers were well into adulthood.

Becoming a teacher, and being given a post of responsibility at such an early age, changed my life completely, and has had the effect over the years of giving me the passion for teaching which I still have. I can't stop myself giving out information/ Not only that, but at the time, with my own days as a pupil still very fresh in my mind, I was able to mentally put myself in the place of the pupils – I had been given the youngest class – and work out ways of getting the message over to them in the most effective way, and this urge to find new and better ways of explaining things has lasted over the years, and ingrained itself in my personal teaching style.

The only other thing which I remember vividly about Sunday School was the annual Sunday School outing. This was always to a local beauty spot, Sutton Park, several miles away. The park was a large expanse of natural countryside with a huge boating lake in it, as well as several different play areas. It was always called "the Sunday School outing", but really it was the opportunity for most of the local congregation to have a day away; in fact, there were so many people who went that they hired a train to take us all there. (This was in the days when there was a very good network of local train lines all over the country, before the dramatic pruning of services by Dr Beeching in 1947.) I suppose these days it is almost inconceivable to imagine a local organisation hiring a whole train for an excursion (unless it is a football club) but then it was quite common.

Digressing completely for a moment, I was brought up in "the Black Country", the heavily industrialised area between Wolverhampton and Birmingham, which was so named because of the dirt and grime caused by smoke on the buildings. On a yearly basis many streets used to have outings where all the men would hire a bus and go off on a day's drinking binge. Having stacked up with many crates of beer, they would start early on a Sunday morning and would stop somewhere for breakfast, (and liquid refreshment,) then carry on for several miles to have lunch, and more refreshment, and the pattern would continue until late into the night, when they would return home, mostly completely incapacitated. Legend says that, arriving back in their own street, they used to knock on the first door, and when the lady of the house appeared at an upstairs window, used to shout, "Missus, come down and pick yowern aht o' we," (yours out of us.)

These days, of course, the coaching industry is much more organised, and lays on a great variety of tours from which one can choose, but when I was young, most coaches belonged to small local companies, and there was far more community spirit, so excursions, by bus or train, were arranged by local groups. However, living in a predominantly working-class area, there was so little in the way of social activities going on that people were *forced* to get together as a community and arrange their own amusements.

It is difficult today to make people understand how different life was back then, immediately after the Second World War. There was no television (I didn't see my first television programme, on a small black-and-white set, until I was eighteen), and cars were a rarity. I knew of only two people who owned cars, one of whom was my uncle, a manager at a local steel works. Some people had radio sets, but reception was very patchy and of poor quality. (We didn't have a set until I was about twelve, which was also the first time that I saw the sea-side). Holidays abroad were a pipe-dream – but in the summer weekly rail excursions to coastal resorts were definitely in fashion.

Every year, most of the local towns had their "Wakes week", which was a time when a fair came, complete with all the excitement of bumping cars, waltzers, shooting galleries, "ghost trains" and the like. For the children there was the added attraction of such gorgeous sweets as candy-floss, which was only ever sold during Wakes week. I can't remember at what time of the year it was, but I suspect it must have been between late autumn and early spring, as it was usually dark in the evenings when we went. However, dark or not, the fairground was always packed with people, enjoying the "once-a-year" event to the full.

Relaxation for men usually consisted of going to the local pub, but of course it would have been unthinkable for a woman to go there – only prostitutes frequented pubs. Even when women started to go to pubs, they couldn't go into the bar; they had to go into the "saloon Bar". I remember the first pub in Wolverhampton which had a "saloon bar"; people used to point it out to their friends, and say, "Look, there's the pub which allows women in".

Transport was very limited, and usually consisted of the local bus services, which were along main roads only, or bicycles, which were plentiful. But people were quite happy walking, even long distances. Very often in the summer, after church, my mother and I – and later my sister as well – used to go for long walks of as far as five miles round the local countryside. (In those days there was a lot of countryside within easy reach of the town, whereas today it has all disappeared into an "urban sprawl" of housing estates.)

People were fiercely parochial, and kept in their own communities without too much mixing with those in others. In the Black Country, there were nineteen very small towns – "Urban Districts" – each of which touched two or three others, so that only the locals knew where the boundaries were. When I married a girl from the next town, a mere two miles away, all the local gossips were saying, "Why does he have to marry a foreigner? Aren't our own girls good enough for him?" (This can be understood today in areas where communities are segregated on racial lines, but in those days there were no immigrants anywhere outside the large cities. I think that I was a teenager before I even *saw* my first black person, and it was even later when I saw my first Asian.) Most people were council tenants, and houses were plentiful. I didn't know anyone in our area who owned their own house, and people in different levels of society lived quite happily together, side by side, which led to greater social cohesion.

Everything has changed over the years; however, the one thing which has changed most dramatically is the attitude towards religion. Most people professed themselves to be Christian, and many made a conscious effort to attend church, if not regularly, at least on the great days in the Christian calendar, Christmas and Easter, when churches would be overflowing.

The manifestation of the Christian faith was celebrated in a very unusual way in our church. Normally, when a minister is appointed to a parish church, he stays there and preaches weekly until he retires, or is moved on to another parish, but in our local church, there was one weekend when a visiting minister was invited to come and take the services. I can't remember what time of the year it was; it might have been late spring or early summer, as the weather was always very warm. (In those days there were no extreme weather conditions such as we see today, and the weather of each season could usually be predicted well in advance.) It could have been scheduled to coincide with the

Christian feast of Pentecost, about seven weeks after Easter, but whenever it was, it happened every year.

The whole weekend was given over to church activities, and was given the appropriate title of "the Sermons weekend". It was the time when everyone put on their best clothes, and in the case of children, it was usually the time when they were bought new clothes to wear. There were organised events over the weekend, including special services and, on the Sunday, a procession of witness through the town and to the local Cenotaph, where a service was held. Most of the congregation joined in this procession, and for the children it was a very exciting time, showing off their newly-acquired finery.

It was also a very important time for the choir, as new music had to be learnt for the special services which were laid on, music which wasn't normally performed at any other time of the year. These pieces of music were in the form of anthems, biblical passages which had been set to music; some of these were quite testing when compared to the standard hymns we usually sang, and needed weeks of additional choir practices to learn. All in all, it was quite an exciting time for us choirboys, and it was made more interesting by the fact that, as the visiting preacher was usually far younger and more energetic than our own decrepit priest, we actually *listened* to what he had to say.

So now, looking back with the benefit of hindsight, how did my childhood shape my religious experiences? Well, quite simply, it indoctrinated me into the virtues of the Christian faith, and taught me that only Christianity was the true religion. (That wasn't very difficult, as I had no knowledge of any of the other world religions, and even the Catholic brand of Christianity was to be shunned.) There was still local animosity between Protestants and Catholics, but it wasn't as bad as in either Northern Ireland or Scotland, as there were so few Catholics in our town. However, near our house there was a Catholic school, and my daily path to school had to cross that of some Catholics going to their school, so we routinely traded insults in passing (always from opposite sides of the road, of course, for safety's sake.)

Spiritually, my early upbringing also gave me a firm foundation of moral values, so by the time that I went to

University I had been so steeped in biblical quotations that I had become conditioned to many of Christianity's ethical concepts.

Before I leave my early years completely, there is one small spiritual incident which perhaps I should mention. I didn't recognise it as a spiritual incident at the time – that came only many years later – but it impressed itself into my mind and is still as clear as ever today.

I must have been very young, perhaps about seven, and had been put to bed with some horrible medicine, probably because I had the beginnings of a cold, or a sniffle. (My mother was a hypochondriac, and was always looking for potential illnesses in my sister and me.) One minute I was just lying in bed and the next I found myself floating round up at ceiling level, looking down at someone lying in bed, (who I didn't realise was me.) This was a lovely feeling of freedom, so I spent some minutes gliding round, twisting and turning to my heart's content, when I suddenly heard my mother's footstep on the stairs.

Terrified that she would look up and see me, and say, "What are you doing up there? Come down this minute." I went and hid in a dark and distant corner of the ceiling. However, I needn't have worried: she just came, looked at the form on the bed and tucked it in, then went out again. Quick as a flash I zoomed down to re-join my body – and woke up.

I now know that I had an "Out-of-Body-experience", where the spirit is for a time separated from (but always loosely joined to) the body, and I know that when in that state it is possible for the spirit to travel anywhere in the universe, in this or the next dimension, and have experiences. I would dearly love to have the ability to do that now, and perhaps one day I will, but it was ironic that my first experience happened when I didn't even recognise what it was.

Chapter Two: Parents

Looking back, more than 35 years after the death of my mother – my father had passed ten years previously – it is difficult to understand how they ever even got together, let alone stayed together. They were so completely different in every way. My father was a highly intelligent man who, born into a different environment, might have risen to a high position as a professional. He was an Aries type, brimming with ideas and – unusually – he also had the practical ability to carry them out. My mother, on the other hand, was a very down to earth Taurean, with not a lot of imagination, and certainly no mental skills to match those of my father, but with an amazing practical ability, particularly where household finances were concerned. He was born into a very poor family, whereas her father was a gifted locksmith engineer, and so on the highest rung of the working-class environment in which they lived. But the yawning gap between them was the question of religion. Both were baptised into the Church of England, but my father had cousins in the Birkenhead area who were – horror of horrors – married to Catholics, and in the eyes of my grandfather, a very bigoted man, that put him definitely "beyond the pale".

I don't know how they met – possibly at some local dance – but she used to say that the first time that she let him "walk her home" they walked on opposite sides of the road – not a good omen for the future. However, both were very good-looking, and my father by that time was quite a smart dresser, so physical attraction was probably what brought them to each other. It must have been a shock when my father was first introduced to his prospective in-laws, and the old man would have definitely fought against the idea of a marriage, but my mother, with Taurean stubbornness, stuck to her guns and eventually got her way, and they were married in October 1924.

Things went wrong from the start. My father had served his time as an apprentice cabinet-maker, and he certainly had a great deal of skill in woodwork. Much later in life, when they were in serious financial difficulties, he made a suite of bedroom furniture from old tea-chests, and that was still in use until 2000, 65 years later. But the economic situation of the country was not good, and father lost his job. He was now in the worst of situations, being under the same roof as, and reliant on hand-outs from, a man who hated him, and who despised him for not being able to maintain his wife. But unexpectedly there was a ray of hope. Although at that time England was in recession, on the other side of the world Australia was booming, and there were several major building projects which were crying out for labour, so a scheme of "assisted passages" was set up to help English workers to emigrate. My father didn't have any money, so most probably the old man subsidised him, obviously hoping that he would never see him again.

As an aside here, my first father-in-law was also attracted to emigrate to Australia at the same time, to work as a skilled boilermaker on the new power station in Victoria, which provided the first mains electricity in the country, and my first mother-in-law always proudly boasted that their house was the first in Australia to have a mains supply. My first wife was born there, and they all came back at about the same time as my father, as the power station had been completed, and all the workers laid off.

But things took an unexpected twist: as Robbie Burns, the Scottish poet said, "The best-laid plans of mice and men gang aft agley" (often go awry). Something amazing happened.

NB: I was completely unaware of this story until after my father's death. His sole surviving sister came to the funeral, and when I took her out for a meal afterwards, before she went home, she told me the saga.

Apparently, my father met someone in Australia, and fell in love with her. Possibly reasoning that he would never be going back to England, he married her, and they had two children, a boy and a girl. However, by 1932, all the major building projects in Australia were coming to an end, and work was very scarce, so the family decided to come to England, and went to live in London.

Learning that I was not my father's first-born was quite an emotional shock to me: somehow it turned my little world upside-down, and meant that what I had always thought as fixed and immutable was now totally false – not a pleasant feeling.

So what led up to my own birth, up in Ellesmere Port, near Birkenhead? Once more, a strange set of events. Apparently, father decided to go back to Willenhall, his home town, to pay a visit to his cousins and bring them up-to-date about his life in Australia, but by misfortune he was seen by a friend of my mother's, who ran across the town to tell her that he was back, and she went and caught him at the house.

This was now disaster: once she knew that he was back, there was no way that he could ever go back to London and resume his life with his (bigamous) wife and family. In fact, to even own up that they existed would make him liable to prosecution; so that was unthinkable, and I don't believe that my mother ever knew all the facts about his return. But worse was to happen, which would put a permanent wedge between my grandfather and my father. My mother became pregnant.

She was now in an impossible position. She could hardly go back to her parents, confess that my father had come back and that she had had secret (and intimate) meetings with him over several months and was now pregnant. They couldn't stay permanently in the house with my father's relatives, as it was too small. So in desperation they decided to go and stay with my father's relatives in Ellesmere Port. However, here we come against what is known as the "Law of Unintended Consequences", as what appeared at first to be a good idea backfired dramatically. Since the only church which was connected to father's family was a Catholic church, I was baptised Catholic, a final insult to my grandfather, and one which he never forgave. In fact, much later in life, when I married for the first time (in a Protestant church), it was seriously suggested that I would first have to be baptised again into the Protestant religion. There was so much heated religious argument about it that eventually the case had to be taken up to the bishop of the local diocese, who fortunately – and sensibly – dismissed the idea out of hand.

They stayed up in Ellesmere Port for the next two years, despite the pleas of my grandma, who wanted to see her first-born grandson, but the matter was eventually settled when my mother became pregnant with my sister, and they finally *had* to go back. Obviously they had to stay with my grandparents, which couldn't have been a very happy situation, but after a couple of years or so they got a council house a short distance away, and that pressure eased.

But the damage had been already done. Over the fifteen years since the wedding, my grandfather's constant invective against my father had had an effect on my mother's attitude towards him, and she started blaming him for everything that went wrong. What is more, she passed this attitude on to her children, and I grew up hating him, as did my sister. In fact, *her* hatred was typified by when she got married, as she banned him from her wedding, and she was "given away" by a friend. Inevitably, in this atmosphere at home, father turned to the only outlet possible – the pub – where he could always be sure of a warm welcome. (In fact, among his fellow-drinkers, he was known as the life and soul of the party).

This wasn't really surprising. I have already mentioned his high intelligence, but he also had a quick wit, and was a brilliant conversationalist. Once more, with the benefit of hindsight, I bitterly regret not having been closer to him, as we could have had some interesting discussions. Very late on in our relationship, we almost had a discussion about Reincarnation, but were interrupted, and the moment was lost.

His intelligence was typified by him leaving school: at that time, the school-leaving age was set at 14, but if a child could pass the school-leaving exam, he/she was allowed to leave earlier. We still have father's leaving certificate, dated on his 13th birthday, so he must have sat and passed the exam while he was still 12. Some accomplishment.

Although his school days were over, his learning wasn't: he became a frequent visitor to the local library, and taught himself bits of a wide variety of subjects, including some Latin phrases.

Parents

(At that time, it was virtually unknown for working-class people to know any Latin, and that situation is probably still true.)

Returning to the subject of my hatred for him, this was cemented by an incident when I was about seven. Father had come back from the pub much worse for wear than normal. He and my mother were having a row, which woke me, and I went to sit on the stairs to listen. Suddenly, I heard a scuffle and my mother shouting, so I ran into the lounge – and found my father trying to strangle her. I ran into the kitchen and got a knife (fortunately just a blunt table-knife,) and stuck it into his ribs. He looked down, saw me and realised what he was doing, and shame-facedly picked me up to comfort me. It never happened again, but for a long time afterwards, after I had gone up to bed each night, I sat on the stairs and waited for my mother to come up, when I crept back into my bed.

It is said that every experience we have is meant as a lesson for us, and this was certainly true in this case. As I have Libra – the peace-lover – rising in my astrological chart, I normally avoid conflict wherever possible, but this incident meant that for the rest of my life I would have a fear of physical violence – in fact, I am quite a coward physically. (That doesn't apply mentally, of course, as I will always "stand my corner" and fight for what I believe in, which has stood me in good stead over the years.)

Now looking at my relationship with my mother, she was a kindly, but firm, disciplinarian; what she said went, and there was no argument possible – in fact, I never even thought about arguing, I just took her word as law. This was shown in a very extreme example when I was seventeen, and about to leave grammar school.

At school I was an average pupil: I could have shone, particularly in Maths, for which I had an affinity, but I was always too lazy to push myself more than by doing what was just acceptable. (This is very often a trait of people with Libra rising.) However, the area in which I excelled was in Languages. I would have liked to specialise in Modern Languages when we had to choose one of four options in the second year at grammar school, either ML, Science, Maths or Classics, but my parents chose Classics, so I studied Latin, Greek and Ancient History up to A

Level. (I had already gained a double-distinction in French at School Certificate Level two years previously.)

So when it was time for me to leave school, I was looking forward to going to University to study languages – but it was not to be. Mother went down to the local market one Saturday morning and saw an old school friend whom she hadn't seen for many years, and they swapped stories and brought each other up to date. Mother asked about the woman's son, Fred, and was told, "Oh, he's doing very well: he's at Birmingham University, studying Law". So when Mother came home, she said to me, "You are going to Birmingham University, to study Law" – and that was that. No consultation, no asking what I wanted to do, or what I was good at; her friend's son was studying Law, so I would be doing that as well. This momentous decision was to lead eventually to me leaving home three years later, as I will explain.

But let me go back a few years: some years earlier, in 1944, a new Education Act had been passed by Parliament, in which grammar schools, of which there were far more than today, were opened up to, and tuition was made free for, all primary school leavers who could pass a standard intelligence test, and I took this the next year, and passed. The local boys' grammar school was in Wolverhampton, three miles away, but at that time there were no defined "catchment areas", so anyone within travelling distance could take the test. I remember that from our school, quite a large junior school, there were several applicants, but only two of us were accepted. (As an aside here, all grammar school were single-sex; such revolutionary ideas as mixed schools were far into the future.)

But although the tuition was now free, nothing else was, and it was necessary for school uniform to be bought, which was a severe strain on any working-class family budget – but somehow Mother managed it. Not only that, two years later, when my sister took the same test and was accepted, she managed to send her to the Wolverhampton Girls" High School.

However, there was more to come: at the end of my first year there was a school trip to Paris, and somehow Mother managed to scrape up enough money to send me on that as well. That eventually proved life-changing for me, as it gave me a love of

France and French, and much later led to me becoming a French interpreter. I have never ceased to have admiration for the way in which she coped financially, but in later life it proved more of a curse than a blessing, as even after there was no need to save, when she could have indulged herself with little luxuries which she had never previously had, she didn't. She hoarded. When eventually we had to clear her flat after her passing, we found 13 big double-blocks of soap, long after she had bought a washing machine and no longer needed them. There was also money stashed away in every corner of the flat, £2,500 in all, which was a small fortune 35 years ago.

So what spiritual lessons did I learn from my parents? Well from my mother, apart from the basic grounding in morals which I have already mentioned, I learnt something about the timing of Death.

It happened like this: every Christmas after my father's death, Mother used to come and stay for the Christmas period with Eleanor and me, so that she could enjoy the excitement of the children when they opened their presents, but one Christmas, in 1984, when I went to fetch her on Christmas Eve she said, "I have decided not to come this year, so I shall just stay at home". I wasn't particularly worried, as she always had enough food in the house to last for a fortnight, but I was shocked when she said to me, just before I left, "I have decided that perhaps it wasn't your Dad's fault".

I couldn't believe my ears: for as long as I could remember she had always been saying that all the problems in the family had been my father's fault, and now she was saying the opposite. So I went back home rather perplexed, and when I told Eleanor she said, "Don't be silly, you must have misheard her." Two days later, on Boxing Day, my sister phoned me to say that she was at Mother's flat, and Mother had collapsed. I dashed over, and held her in my arms, waiting for the ambulance to arrive, but by the time it did it was too late – she had already passed.

So what did that teach me? Well, it taught me that each of us comes into life to learn certain lessons, and that no-one will leave their life before those lessons are learnt. My mother had to learn that there are two sides to every story, and until she had done that, she wasn't *allowed* to go home. By not coming home with me, she had given herself time over Christmas to really think about her relationship with my father, and had at last come to terms with it, and learned the lesson.

Another thing that I learnt was the meaning of the word "soul mates". In popular terms, this means two people coming together in perfect harmony, and living a life of bliss, without any problems, but I believe that is totally false. Going on the premise that we all come into life to learn lessons, what possible gain could we get from such a relationship – we would learn nothing at all. To refer back to my parents, they had fought like cat and dog all their life, and when they got into their mid-60s, they were both so tired of fighting that they gave up – and entered the most wonderful period of their married life. They became almost "Darby and Joan" figures, and began to even speak of each other affectionately. After my father had passed, to hear mother speaking of him, any outsider would have thought that they had had a lifetime of bliss, which they certainly hadn't. So perhaps "soul mates" refers to two people who come together and fight through all the obstacles in order to finally reach a harmonious relationship together.

There are obvious exceptions to this, of course. Where two highly-developed spiritual people come together, it may be that instead of learning lessons themselves they are here to teach others, or to do some high-level spiritual work. However, I think that this proves to be the exception, rather than the rule.

As I said, in my early years I hated my father, but in later years I mellowed towards him, and after his passing regretted not having been able to get closer. I often thought about his life, but could never understand why he had been so antagonistic to my mother. She provided a good home for him, and certainly managed the family finances brilliantly. Of course, she had been conditioned against him by her father, and it didn't help that her elder sister, Mary, had married George Wilcox, a rising star in the local steel works. (He eventually became a director.) He was a pillar of the local church, the scout master, and never smoked or drank, so the differences between him and my father were obvious. However, that still didn't explain the antagonism, and the puzzle wasn't eventually solved until a couple of months ago when there was an incident.

I was thinking about him and trying to get into his mind-set, when suddenly I felt an overwhelming sadness, and broke down in tears. I sobbed uncontrollably for several minutes, completely against my stoical Aquarian character, and then I was given a scenario which could explain his whole life, as follows:

He never truly loved my mother, as most of the initial attraction had been physical (with possibly a touch of "making a good marriage" as well), and very soon after they moved in with my grandparents he found what a big mistake he had made. However, there was no way of getting out of the marriage; divorce was virtually impossible in those days, and even if it had been available, the cost would have made it prohibitive for any but the wealthy. So he was stuck, and when he had the chance of going to Australia he welcomed it with open arms.

He had a varied time in Australia, doing whatever casual work was available, and spent some time as a "swagman", of the kind in the "Waltzing Matilda" song. But then he moved to an area where there was a lot of work, probably Sydney, where the bridge was being built, and settled down, and it was at that time that he met the love of his life.

I have no information at all about the lady in question, but I am going to call her "Mary", for the sake of reference. I don't know how long the courtship lasted, as in those days quick marriages were definitely not in fashion, but eventually marry they did, and Mary produced a boy and a girl.

However, the good times were coming to an end, and work was drying up. Once the Sydney Harbour Bridge was finished, a huge number of men were thrown out of work, so there were no further prospects in Australia, and they decided to come to England. He couldn't afford to buy tickets for all of them, so he paid for "Mary" and the children, and worked his own passage back as a deck hand. One of my daughters, who now lives in Australia, has been able to verify this in local records. They got back to England some time in 1932, and settled in London, and then father made the biggest mistake in his life – he decided to go back to Willenhall to visit his cousins, and tell them of his news.

They lived in a poorer part of the town, so he thought that there was no danger of meeting anyone whom my mother knew – but he was wrong. He was seen, my mother was told, and he was caught, and could never go back.

For the rest of his life he bitterly regretted his mistake; he hated my mother's nosey friend, and he resented my mother – but most of all he grieved. He grieved for the loss of his only true love, and that of his children, whom he loved dearly, and he grieved for the realisation that there would never be any possibility of being able to turn the clock back and relive the happiness which he had found in Australia. The grief was similar to that for a departed loved one, but much worse in the long run. After a time, the departed loved one finds a way of impressing those left behind with his presence, and the grieving lightens somewhat. (This is the reason behind the saying, "Time is a great healer.") But for my father, there was no such possibility: he was stuck. However, I believe that there was a time when he tried to go back, many years later, during the war.

He had a protected occupation as a steelworker in the local steelworks, so he didn't have to enrol for military service, but at that time many ships in trans-Atlantic convoys were getting destroyed by German U-Boats, and there was a need for seamen. As father had had experience as a deckhand, one day he packed his big seaman's trunk, and announced that he was going to volunteer in Liverpool, the main trans-Atlantic port – but after a week he was back, saying that there were no ships waiting in the port. I have always wondered about that, as with a port of that size there would always be a need for seamen on one ship or another. So did he go to Liverpool, or go the other way, and try to find his long-lost family in London. I will never know, but if he *had* found his family, and had been reunited with them, it would certainly have been a very good way of moving out of my mother's life. His disappearance would have been understood as "Lost at Sea."

So the outcome of this is that there is quite possibly a family called Steadman somewhere in London, who have a legend in their family history of an ancestor who went to the Midlands on a short visit and never came back. It is unlikely that either of my two half-siblings (could my half-brother have been named

"Ralph"?) are still alive, as both would be in their late eighties now, but some of their descendants might still be around. If so, it might comfort them to know that father loved their grandmother deeply until the very end of his life.

So my mother was on a hiding to nothing in her marriage: she was with a man who was deeply grieving for a "Mary", of whose existence she didn't even know, and she could never do anything to improve the situation. Many years later, when father was on his deathbed, I was sitting with him and saw that he was deep in thought, with a wistful look on his face. I like to think that he was re-living the wonderful days with "Mary" in Australia, before everything went wrong.

So, in conclusion, what have I leaned from my relations with my father? Well, the first, and possibly the most important thing on a personal basis, is not to let gossip, or the views of others, colour your own opinions about someone's character – and this is particularly true in reverse if you are a parent. Do not make your children hate the other parent. My relationship with my father was irrevocably poisoned by my mother's thoughts about him, and yet I am sure that I missed a great deal in my early days by not being willing to learn from him. Parents, teach your children moral principles by all means, but don't use them as a weapon against anyone else, least of all the other parent.

Next, if you feel antagonism towards another, try to understand the position they are in. If I had known my father's true situation, I would never have behaved towards him in the way I did. However, as I have explained, when I finally realised it, it was all too late.

The final thing I learnt is a deeply spiritual lesson. When I eventually learned (and *felt*) the depth of his grief, I found myself almost wishing that he hadn't made his big mistake, and gone back to Willenhall at that fateful time – but then, on reflection, I realised what would have happened. He himself would have had a loving life in London with "Mary" and his family, but neither my sister nor I, nor our 28 direct descendants, would have ever been born. Most of those descendants have now grown up and become "worthy citizens", and some have made dramatic – and beneficial – changes in the lives of many in their local environment. So I believe that my father's "mistake" wasn't a mistake at all – it was fated to happen. In other words, it was **predestined**.

There have always been arguments in spiritual circles about the conflict between Free Will – where each soul has complete choice over the conditions in his life, and Predestination, where everything is planned in advance, and I had faced this dilemma many years before when dealing with Reincarnation, and had solved the problem, reconciling the two opposites in a logical way, although everyone won't agree with me. I explain my philosophy on Predestination in a later chapter. I found that my father's life was an extreme example of the interaction of both principles. He made the deliberate choice to go back to Willenhall (Free Will) and then was hit by the consequences, (Predestination).

Chapter Three: University

The next three years of my life were a strange mixture. They were spent as a day student at Birmingham University, in the Faculty of Law – at least, they were *supposed* to have been spent there. The Faculty of Law was housed in an old building in the centre of the city, whereas most of the other faculties had already been housed in the modern new campus in Selly Oak, an open suburb a couple or so miles out of the city. I say *supposed* to have been spent, as the majority of my time was spent either in the large common room, playing bridge, or in a tiny room up in the attics, playing table-tennis. This was because I hated the course which I was on, I resented having to study something which had no attraction for me whatsoever, and I was determined to show my disapproval by doing as little work as possible to get through.

Socially, those years were a great eye-opener. Brought up in a fairly sheltered atmosphere, in a working-class district far from any city glamour, I now found myself with an education grant from the local authority which was far more money than I had ever owned in my life, and the freedom to travel back and forth on railways, which I had hardly ever known. I started to smoke and got a taste for "scrumpy", a particularly wicked form of still cider which was aptly nick-named "falling-down-water". It was so sweet and bland that, when you were drinking it, it slid down like water, but when you tried to walk afterwards, you fell down. There were very few adolescents in our area who were at University, so both my parents were very proud of the fact that I was, and never ceased to brag about the fact to their friends. (My father always used to say that I was at the "Varsity", which was quite wrong, as in those days that term should have been used for only Oxford or Cambridge, but he didn't mind.) These days, of course, there are so many universities that it is almost *expected* that most youngsters with high education qualifications will go to one, but those days were far in the future in 1951.

As part of my social education I met students from all over the country, and became firm friends with a few of them. None of them were really "upper-class", but the majority were "middle-class", and so seemed very grand to someone of my background. This gave me a first impression of what life was like in other environments, which was to prove a fore-runner for the far greater – and far more brutal – shock of National Service later on.

Spiritually it was a strictly "non-event" period. By that time I was a more-or-less hardened Christian, but I didn't join the Christian Society, and I still attended church back home at the weekends, but nothing happened to either forward my knowledge or to challenge my beliefs. All that was to come later. However, there was one major life-changing event which did happen during my first year as a student: I met my future wife. I had met a group of friends to play tennis on the local council courts, and she happened to be there with a group of her friends, so our paths crossed. She came from a similar background to me, and was a student-teacher in her last year at college, so we got on very well, and slipped into a relationship almost without knowing it.

But Nemesis was approaching, in the form of my final year at University, and I was at last forced to do some work, and realised with horror how much I had to catch up on. So Finals exams came and went, and all of the undergraduates were de-briefed about their results. My tutor told me that the teaching staff had had a long talk about me, and someone had said that he *thought* that there was a *possibility* that I *might* eventually, after many years, make a lawyer, so on that basis they had decided to award me a "Pass" degree, the lowest possible grade. So in July 1954, at a ceremony attended by my father and Eleanor, my girl-friend, I became an LL.B. (Bachelor of Law and Logic.)

Incidentally, that was the first of three professional qualifications which I got in my life – the others were in Teaching and Linguistics, as a French interpreter. So wherever I went wrong in life, it couldn't have been through a lack of intelligence. However, intelligence and common sense are not the same thing, as my two beloved wives found out to their dismay. Eleanor worshipped intelligence – one of the things which attracted her to me in the first place was the fact that I was at University, and she didn't know any other undergraduates – but in later life she had to ruefully admit that she had married an "educated idiot".

In my old age, I am so useless from a point of practical work that if my beloved second wife Sybil sees me with a screwdriver in my hand, she tells me to go and lie down until the urge to try and use it has gone away. I myself have always rated intelligence very highly on the scale of human accomplishments but today, with many decades of hind-sight, I think that in my next incarnation I will choose a life as a "village idiot", who knows nothing but who can do everything.

I said earlier that going to University would be the cause of me leaving my parental home permanently, and so it proved to be. This is how it happened:

In those days there was a national scheme which was called National Service, under which every young man aged 18 had to register to serve two years in one of the military services, Army, Navy or Air Force. There were few exceptions to the rule, but one was that if you were following a course of study, you could claim yearly exemptions until it ended, when you were conscripted. After my degree I could have applied for an "apprenticeship", articled to a local solicitor, but that would have meant being tied into years of work in a profession which I hated. So I deliberately refrained from applying anywhere until after the final date for deferment had passed, after which the wheels of officialdom swung into action, and I was called up – and my fate was sealed.

So my years at University had provided an easy and interesting period which slid me from my childhood years, living in the parental home, into full adulthood and the new adventures which awaited me – including, of course, the start of my spiritual life. Three years previously I had gone there as a very naïve seventeen-year-old; now I had matured into a far more worldly-wise character, but that process was about to accelerate more rapidly than I could ever have imagined.

Chapter Four:
Army Life - Training

As I said earlier that going to University was an eye-opener for me, as it allowed me to mix with people from a different background, but that was nothing like the shock of becoming a soldier, when I met the full spectrum of backgrounds, from very poor to extremely rich. I was first sent to Aldershot, to a basic training camp where we were taught the rudiments of how to look after ourselves, keep clothes and equipment clean, make beds, lay out kit for inspections, drill and – above all – submit to discipline. The latter was all-important, and over-rode everything else, and the whole aim of that first fortnight was to break the spirit of anyone who had the slightest idea of not conforming. The "little tin gods" who were entrusted with this vital task were the corporals, who had absolute power over recruits, and could dish out the most demeaning of tasks at will. For instance, one "cocky" recruit was given a pair of nail scissors and sent outside to cut the lawn, and told not to come back till he had done so. A couple of hours later he was actually allowed back, as it was tea-time, but he never crossed that particular corporal again.

The extent of the terror which the corporals created was shown in one small incident during our second week. We had been marched down to the camp barber's shop for the *third* time, and stood down outside waiting to be called in, so the corporal said, "You can all smoke." No-one moved a muscle, as we had all been forbidden to smoke since we arrived, and to be told the opposite now didn't make sense. However, the corporal, seeing that no-one was moving, snarled, "I said SMOKE..." Even people who had never smoked in their life were begging smokers for a cigarette, just so that they could obey.

Army Life - Training

The official reason for the first fortnight was for recruits to be selected to go to different destinations, and be medically tested for possible problems. Everyone had been given a choice of three different careers in the paperwork that had been sent to them before they arrived at the camp, and because of my background I had chosen 1) Education Corps, 2) Intelligence Corps and 3) Pay Corps. The Army authorities, in their wisdom, had assigned me to the Service Corps.

During my personal interview with a Selection Officer I was asked if I would like to apply for a commission, for which my degree qualified me, but I declined. I often wonder what my life would have been like had I accepted – certainly much different – but I took the decision and I had to live with the consequences. (Another example of Free Will, leading on to Predestination.) So then I was asked what side of the Service Corps I would like to serve in, Clerical or Driving. Well, I didn't fancy a desk job – I had walked away from the choice of office work already – so I asked for Driving, as at least that would give me a skill which would be useful in the future, and in due course I was sent to a Driver Training School, in Yeovil, Somerset.

There were two massive Army camps in Yeovil at the time, Houndstone, which was for basic training, and Lufton, which was a "holdee" camp for trained drivers awaiting posting to one of the dozens of places throughout the world needing drivers. So I spent my next eight weeks in Houndstone, learning to be a driver. The regime was relatively relaxed, certainly compared with what I had experienced in Aldershot. We still had parades, and 'square-bashing", which is marching up and down and learning to act together as a squad, rather than as individuals – but the rest of the time was spent in lectures and demonstrations of how engines work, and in training runs out into the beautiful Somerset countryside round Yeovil. I was an eager learner but – with my lack of practical skills – didn't make very rapid progress. In fact, I didn't pass my test until the third attempt, which knocked my instructor's averages down a bit.

Nothing spiritual happened during my time in Yeovil, but I did certainly learn a few social skills, including how to relate to people from totally different backgrounds. I can't remember more than

33

about ten of my fellow recruits, but some of the ones I do remember came from such varied backgrounds as "Dundee", a fish–filleter from Dundee, (we never found out his real name), Bill, a gentle soul from the Gorbals in Glasgow, Don, a wall-of-death motor-cyclist from Southport, "scouse", an Irish prize-fighter from Liverpool, Pete, a farm-worker from Norfolk, Bob, an accountant from Essex, and another Don, the son of a wealthy sausage-maker in London. I was instantly nicknamed "the Professor", or "Prof" for short, as I was the only one who had been to University, and I was often asked to read letters, or write letters home, for comrades who could do neither.

I was also able to use a bit of social psychology to my advantage. It happened this way:

Once a week, on a Friday morning, we had a camp inspection, so Thursday evenings were marked down for "Household Economy", a posh name for working to make sure that the whole of the barrack block was bright and shining and ready for the next morning. There was a whole range of jobs which had to be done, from polishing the floors and sponging down walls to cleaning windows, dusting surfaces, cleaning washrooms and tidying up outside. There was a graduation of jobs, some of which were very easy and quickly done, while others were long and tedious. The worst of the lot was "Clean the toilets".

The first night I analysed all the jobs to be done, and then the second week, when the corporal asked for volunteers for the toilets, I put my hand up, and did the job. The next week was the same, and the corporal looked at me strangely, before almost reluctantly assigning the job to me. But the third week, when I volunteered again, he hesitated; trying to work out what it was that was attracting me to the job. Finally, he gave up, and chose someone else. I was left to the end, to do the easiest job of all, "Company runner", which meant that if there were any messages that had to be sent to anyone, (a very unlikely event,) I would take them. And so it worked out for the rest of the time there – I always volunteered for the worst job but got the best, as the corporal never quite understood my "angle" in volunteering.

At the end of the course we all "graduated" as drivers, and got transferred to Lufton, over the road, to the "holdee" camp. Life here was relatively easy, as apart from a couple of parades a day, the odd bit of drill and occasional training rides out into the countryside, to maintain our driving skills, there was virtually nothing to do. Most people were there for only a very short time, as there was a continuous call for drivers to be posted out, but this was not for me. One of the least-liked chores was working in the kitchens, as a general dogs-body. It involved getting up very early in the morning to start work at 6.00 a.m., but one was excused all parades, and was free for the rest of the day after lunch. So once again, I volunteered, and spent several weeks there. The work wasn't strenuous; mostly it involved either preparing vegetables or putting dirty crockery onto the giant revolving washing machine and stacking the clean items at the other end. However, there were perks: the kitchen staff was always the best fed, and late at night, if we ever wanted a "fried-egg sarnie", we could always go to the back door of the kitchen and get the duty cook to knock us one up.

However, my life was about to take another turn. There was a small Education Centre in Lufton Camp, to provide education and run exams for the large number of permanent staff on the two camps, and one day a volunteer was asked for, to work at the centre, doing odd jobs, and I put my hand up. I was immediately taken back mentally to my Sunday school teacher days, and very soon made myself as useful as possible, to the delight of the two corporals who did most of the day-to-day work there. In fact, they were so impressed after I had been there for two or three days that they asked the Major in charge if I could be seconded permanently, and I was.

I was now in my seventh heaven of delight, and rapidly wormed my way into doing actual *teaching*. The system was that in order to be promoted, every non-officer rank was supposed to have passed one of a series of examinations. The lowest level, Army Certificate of Education 3, (ACE3), was little more than a basic writing and arithmetic test, but it was needed for promotion to Lance-Corporal. The second level, ACE2, which was a bit harder, involved English and Maths and a sketchy knowledge of Current Affairs, and was needed for promotion to Sergeant, while the top one, ACE1, involved English, Maths, and Map-reading. It was needed for promotion to Warrant Officer, and was somewhere near the level of the current GCSE grade C.

Well, this was only a few years after the end of the second World War, and during the war people had been promoted on merit, without thought of educational qualifications, and there was now a huge need of "catching-up" education to be done, so although the centre was only small, a major, a lieutenant, two corporals and me, there were always courses going on. I quickly proved my worth and was soon teaching ACE3 and Maths and English at ACE2, to the delight of everyone concerned. This eventually led me to asking for an interview with the Major, to probe the possibilities of transferring to the Royal Army Educational Corps, (RAEC), and to him recommending me.

I left Yeovil in spring 1955, just after the most important event in my life, my marriage to Eleanor. We had been "courting" for a long while, but there had been no possibility of marriage before I got my degree, and then I was away in the Army; but we were eventually married on 16th April 1955, and on our wedding certificate my profession was given as "Driver, R.A.S.C." However, it was to be almost a year before we would be able to live together.

My new life was very pleasant, and certainly a step up in quality from life at Yeovil. First of all, instead of living in a dormitory and socialising in a crowded N.A.A.F.I., I was in a room with two other students, and socialised in the Sergeants' Mess, much the disgust of most of the permanent staff there; they had reached their rank through the normal lengthy channels, taking many years, whereas we, the students, would be given the rank of Sergeant at the end of our 6-month course.

The course passed quickly enough: it was a potted course, designed as a smaller version of the standard Teacher Training course in civilian life, and containing all the usual things of educational psychology lectures, practice lessons, lesson plans, and the like, but slanted towards the needs of the three Army certificates. We also had a lot of Map-reading instruction, as this was completely new to most students, whereas all would have already studied English and Maths to a fairly high level at school.

Army Life - Training

I was looking forward to graduating in October, but then I had a great shock. I was called in to see the course tutor one day, and he asked me how I had found the course. I said that I had really enjoyed it, and was looking forward to going out "into the field" and being posted to a unit where I could practise what I had learnt, when he said, "Well, we have a bit of a problem there. You might not be able to do that." I was staggered, but he explained that it was an Army rule that no National Service sergeant could graduate from the course if he had less than 12 months of service left to do – and I would have only 11 months. So I had the choice of either being sent back to Yeovil as an RASC driver again, or signing on for a further three years as a regular soldier.

Well, this was a "no-brainer" really. There was no way at all that I was going to leave the comfort of a Sergeants' Mess and return to the life (and salary) of a driver, so I asked for a weekend leave pass to go home and consult my wife. The tutor agreed, and that weekend we decided that I should enlist. So I did, graduated as a sergeant and a few months later, in early 1956, I was posted to my first unit, a Royal Electrical and Mechanical Engineers (REME) depot in Sudbury, Staffordshire. This move was about to provide my first ever message from a Spiritualist medium.

At that time, Eleanor was still living with her parents in Bilston, now a suburb of Wolverhampton. I was free from duty at midday every Saturday, so I used to wait outside the camp for the little bus which trundled round the country villages on its way to Burton-on-Trent, where I caught a train to Birmingham, another to Wolverhampton, and then a local bus to Bilston. I always arrived at my parents-in-law's house at about the same time every week.

This Saturday, early in March 1956, I was waiting at the bus-stop when a friend from the Mess pulled up in his car and asked me if I wanted a lift. I said that I was going to Burton, and he said that he could take me part of the way there, to a small village called Tutbury, through which my bus would have to pass; I accepted, and he took me there.

However, I realised that I hadn't actually gained anything at all by accepting the lift; I still had to wait for the same bus, but now wait for longer, while it visited all the little villages, so I went into the local pub and had a pint. I asked if the landlord knew of any local lodgings, as I had just been posted to Sudbury, and he pointed out the house opposite, where there were rooms vacant. I went to see the owner, saw the rooms, and agreed to take them, subject to my wife's approval. It was then time to cross the street back to the bus-stop, as the bus was slowly chugging up the hill. I caught the same trains and bus as usual, and got to the house at the same time as normal.

When I got there, the small kitchen was crammed with people, as "Auntie Margaret" was reading the cards. Auntie Margaret, my wife's aunt, was a very powerful medium, who had at one time served on the prestigious Marylebone Circuit in London, the most famous Spiritualist circuit in the world, but had now come back to the Midlands and was running a church held in a local community centre.

I stood for a while by the door, not saying a word, and mentally scorning these gullible people listening to a load of old rubbish from a silly old woman. When she had finished with all of them, she turned to me and asked if I would like a reading. I scornfully refused, but Eleanor "gave me the eye" and said, "Sit down." So I did.

The first words she said to me were, "You are going to live in that house you have been to see. They are nice people, and they have a little boy. Eleanor will work at that school, and be interviewed by three men. You will be very happy in the house, but will live there only one year exactly." Everyone was amazed, and wanted to know where I had been, and Eleanor was particularly impressed. After all, we had been married for almost a year without living together, so she wanted to have her own home and – most of all – have her first child. So it was arranged that she should go over to see the house the next weekend. She did, liked it, so we moved in on March15th, 1956.

Everything happened exactly as Auntie Margaret had predicted. Eleanor applied for a job at the school, and was told that she would be interviewed by two men, but when she turned up there was a third one there, who was introduced as a visiting schools inspector and who, "by coincidence", was paying an unscheduled visit that day. We were very happy there, and – happiest of all – she found that she was pregnant. The old saying is, "A new house, a new baby", and we certainly moved house several times during our marriage. In the early months of the marriage, Eleanor used to cry every month when she found that she *wasn't* pregnant. In later years, I think that she cried every time when she found out that she *was*, as we eventually had six children. All of them were deeply loved, of course, but it must have been quite a shock to her each time, particularly when things weren't going smoothly in the marriage.

Then, on March 1st 1957, while I was away, the landlord called her in and said that his brother had died, and the sister-in-law would be coming to live with them, and would need our rooms. He gave Eleanor a fortnight's notice and she left on March 15th, exactly a year to the day after having moved in, as predicted by Auntie Margaret.

Chapter Five:
Army Life - Later Days

I would prefer to miss out the next episode, which was very painful, but I mustn't, as it had several important effects, and set the scene for my later Army life. At Sudbury I thoroughly enjoyed myself, and so did Eleanor. We were young, in our first home together, and had a wonderful social life in the Sergeants' Mess. When Michael, our first son, was born, life was perfect; what could possibly go wrong?

What went wrong, and spoilt everything, was that I had a talk with my officer one day, and he persuaded me to apply for a commission, which I did. I attended a residential selection course, which I passed, and in spring 1957 I went away to Eaton Hall, near Chester, for Officer Training. But before I talk about that, I will mention another spiritual lesson which concerned our time at Sudbury.

Twenty or more years after I had left the army I happened to be passing through Staffordshire on my way to the north of England, when I decided to make a detour and visit the army camp which held so many lovely memories for us. I located it on the map and drove there, expecting to see some of the buildings which had been on the huge, sprawling camp, but was amazed to find nothing but empty fields, with only one building, which might have once been the Officers' Mess, sitting forlornly in the middle.

This taught me a lesson: whatever happens to us in life, and whatever happy memories we have of any place, they are best left like that, just memories, because if we return to visit the scene much later, we will find that everything has changed. Buildings we once knew and loved will have either been demolished or renovated, new buildings will be everywhere, and even whole streets may well have disappeared. I lived in Wolverhampton for many years, but the last time that I went there I got lost in the rebuilt town centre, with its new roads and buildings. The Romans had a phrase for it: "*Tempora mutantur, et nos mutamur in illis*", (times change, and we change with them,) and that is so very true.

Now about Eaton Hall: I had thought it might be something like my time at Wilton Hall, the RAEC training depot, but how wrong I was. It was a school for training infantry officers, and was physically and mentally tough.

Had I gone there directly from Aldershot, I might have survived, but after more than a year in the laid-back surroundings of two Sergeants' Messes, I had no chance, as I was physically unfit and had started to get a "senior rank mentality", which didn't do me any good at all, or help me to knuckle down to the status of a trainee once more.

The final test was a fortnight at Battle Camp, near Trawsfynnyth, in Wales, where we were put through a series of extreme tests. I think that the moment I realised that this was not for me was when I saw a section leader, up to his neck in muddy water, shouting, "Come on, men; follow me." When we returned to Eaton Hall after that fortnight, I was summoned before the Commanding Officer, told that I was not suitable to be an infantry officer, and would be returned to my unit – the dreaded RTU. In that appalling psychological atmosphere, that weekend, our second son was conceived.

However, despite the massive blow to my ego, this event was to be the first of several in my spiritual life which proved that everything, eventually, happens for our spiritual benefit, although we may not see it as such at the time. I returned to Wilton Park, but found that I now had a new status. Previously, I had been, in the eyes of many of the permanent staff – the "old sweats" in the Sergeants' Mess – a mere National Service upstart, but now I was a "returnee" a fully-fledged regular sergeant who had come back to the depot to await his next posting, and so was accepted as a true "senior rank". I got there in early July 1957, and for the next month there was very little to do, just the occasional guard duty.

However, never in my wildest dreams could I have imagined what was to come next.

One day the postings officer called me into his office and asked me how good my French was and I answered that it was very good, (thinking back to my double-distinction in French at School Certificate, eight years earlier). So he said to me, "Good – how would you like to go to NATO, in France?" How would I like to? This was one of the most sought-after postings in the world, so I assured him that I would love it, and be able to cope with the language, and it was settled there and then. So the next month I found myself in a small unit of one Warrant Officer and another sergeant, in the British Army Camp Support Unit, in Fontainebleau. My wife and son joined me a month or so later, and our second son, Robert, was born in the local hospital the following spring. So began the happiest three years of our early married life, before things started to go wrong.

It is difficult to explain how incredibly rich we were during our time in France. At that time, every serviceman and woman had a basic wage, which was paid, net of tax, over the pay-table weekly, but that was only the start of the matter; the average cost of living in the host country was calculated, and measured against the cost of living in the UK, and if there was any higher difference it was paid as an extra tax-free allowance, a Local Overseas Allowance, (LOA). Now at that time, only twelve years after the end of the war, the cost of living in France was much higher than that in the UK, so a huge amount of LOA was added to each wage-packet, which meant that my weekly wage was something like four times that of the average adult male worker in the UK at the time. In spending power that was the equivalent of a weekly wage of about £1,000 in today's money – but even that was only half of the story.

NATO had set up what was known as "the SHAPE Shop", (SHAPE was short for Supreme Headquarters Allied Powers in Europe,) which all NATO personnel were automatically allowed to use – and everything sold in the shop was free of tax. Any brand of cigarettes, for instance, was 5p for 20 in today's money, and a bottle of whisky was only 38p.

So we had unimaginable spending power. We immediately bought a new car, of course, as everyone did. Ours was a right-hand-drive Morris Oxford, which cost us all of £389 – nine weeks' wages – and we rented half of a house in a neighbouring village, for which we paid about £17 a month rent. (For an extra £5 a month we could have rented a big detached house, but we didn't fancy that.) All the rest was free spending money – and did we spend. It was always, "Go for the best of everything, no matter what the price." So we lived very well indeed, with no thought for the future.

For the first nine months or so, we lived in the village, which was about five miles from Fontainebleau, so we were a bit separated from the main social life of the Unit, but then, having never had an official "Married Quarters", I was allocated a flat in a luxury international forces block in the middle of Fontainebleau, and we could join in everything fully. "A new house, a new baby" – and David, our second French son was born in 1959.

Life was very good; we had a large number of friends, including American and Canadian families, there was a "Club Femotan" – a women's club which provided lots of social gatherings for the wives, and plenty of entertainment for the children, during the day while the husbands were at work – and there was a massive Bingo every Friday night. (If you weren't in at least an hour before the start, you wouldn't get a seat.) No wonder it was so popular – the weekly top prize was a big saloon car. We had a ball.

From a work point of view life wasn't very strenuous. The job of the British Support Unit was to back up those who worked in the NATO offices as clerks or interpreters, so most were highly skilled and qualified, and didn't need to do Army exams; for the lower ranks, the drivers, cooks and general duties people, there was a fairly stable workforce, with little or no promotion possible, so there was no need for Education classes. Therefore the RAEC staff was normally used as unofficial interpreters, helping families to move in or out of lodgings, and conducting negotiations with local French landlords. We also helped to arrange social evenings and outings, and liaised with French sports teams to arrange "international" football or hockey matches.

I was quickly "thrown into the deep end" as an interpreter, and soon learnt that French, as taught in grammar school, was quite different to what was spoken in the country by the natives. So I had to learn a lot, very quickly. However, things did not always go smoothly. Sometimes we were called in to try to pacify angry landlords and tenants when disputes arose, and this often called for extreme diplomacy. A typical conversation might go like this:

"Tell this thieving Froggie landlord that it is time he did some maintenance around the place". Translation: "The British gentleman believes that there is some maintenance needed."

"Tell the bastard that if his out-of-control hooligan brats didn't smash the place up so much, there would be a lot more money to do repairs." Translation: "The French gentleman believes that possibly some damage has been caused by your children."

And so the conversation would go on, with me skating on thin ice trying to maintain the peace. Usually I was successful, and managed to restore harmony, but there were occasions when eventually both parties turned on me and seemed to blame me for everything.

On a happier note, I became very friendly with the two French ladies who were cooks in the unit, and had the interesting experience of introducing them to our national dish of "fish and chips". They first had to learn the difference between chips and French fries, which wasn't too difficult, but the big stumbling block was the idea of actually *frying* fish, which they couldn't understand at all. So I had to patiently take them through the process bit by bit. They were very dubious until they tasted the result of their first attempt, but after that they became firm believers, and from that time onwards "feesh and sheeps" was always on the menu.

However, for us domestically there was one small "fly in the ointment" which was to have severe implications later in life, although we didn't know it at the time. Robert, our second son, had word dyslexia, which meant that he wasn't able to completely hear and understand language. Therefore he was very slow to start talking, and when he did talk it was in an unintelligible jabber. This wasn't helped by the fact that he heard children speaking in other languages, which confused him even more, so until he was about 18-months-old the only person who could understand him was Michael, then three.

The situation was solved in a very interesting way. We enrolled the children in a small kindergarten for British children in town, run by Miss Liddell, a typical 'spinster schoolmistress", who terrorised everyone, French and English alike. (To hear her swearing in fluent French at unfortunate tradesmen who incurred her wrath was a frequent "crowd spectacle".) She very soon realised what the problem was between Robert and Michael, and immediately solved it – by putting them in separate groups. Within a fortnight Robert was speaking intelligible English.

However, in among all this apparent happiness, cracks were starting to appear in our marriage, and these were because of the difference in our respective characters. Eleanor was always very cautious and careful, particularly with money, as she had been brought up in a very deprived area of the country, where every penny counted, whereas I was a stubborn man who couldn't see any further than my own nose – and certainly didn't believe in saving for a rainy day. I was enjoying all my new-found wealth while I could. Many of the men on the camp were buying homes on a mortgage in the UK, and were able to pay off most of their loans during their three-year posting in France, and Eleanor begged me to do the same – but I wouldn't listen. It came to a crunch when her parents" small two-bed roomed house came onto the market, at the princely price of £600, and I refused to even think about buying it, much to Eleanor's disgust. (At that time, £600 represented less than fourteen weeks' wages.) What a fool I was. This was a pattern which repeated itself for the next twenty-five years, us arguing about money, and me being proved wrong every time. I did eventually learn the lesson, but regrettably far too late in life.

So what did my time in France teach me? Well, spiritually, nothing. Socially, it made me a very fluent French speaker, which was of enormous value to me in later (civilian) life, but it also gave me an over-inflated sense of my own importance, a disregard of common-sense spending habits, and an addiction to smoking and drinking – not good omens for the future.

However, "all good things come to an end", and now it was time for a bit of harsh reality to be injected into my life. After three glorious years in France, I was posted to Malta, where conditions were so different it was almost like being in a different world. Climate, work, social life, and the harsh exposure to the idiocy and corruption of the local Government bureaucracy were a great shock to the system, and this started on the very first day that we arrived. We had driven down from France, through Italy and Sicily, and had taken a tiny little boat called "The Star of Malta" overnight to the island. The boat was so small that there was room for only two cars on the deck, so I locked all the car documents in the car and handed over the keys to the deck hand in charge. When we arrived in Valetta Harbour the next morning, we found that the car had already been unloaded, and taken to the car pound on the quayside, so we went along to the office to register our arrival and reclaim the car. That was the start of my introduction to crazy Maltese officialdom.

I was asked for the number of the car, and then its documentation. I said that this was in the car, and asked for the keys to go and get it. This was not possible, I was told, as the regulations said that I couldn't be given the keys until I had provided the documentation, so no documentation, no keys. But without the keys, I couldn't get the documentation. I asked to be escorted by an official to the car so that *he* could get the documentation, but that wasn't allowed, either. It was a complete "catch-22" situation, and I was sent away without the car to the Army unit to which I was being posted. I reported in and we were lodged in temporary accommodation in a hotel, pending arrangements for us to get to get permanent lodgings.

Three weeks later we were still in a stalemate, but now things were getting desperate. Living in a hotel room, with three small children, and no change of clothing for anyone, was taking its toll, so as a last resort I went to see my Colonel and explained the situation. He said, "Come with me.", and his driver took us to the port. He marched up to the desk, where a sleepy-eyed clerk sprang to attention and saluted, and then he said, "I need some important military documents out of car No ....." "Certainly sir", said the clerk, and handed over the keys without question. We went to the pound and got the documents, and then the Colonel asked if I had any electronic apparatus, which apparently attracted enormous import duty. I said that I had, a latest 'state-of-the-art' hi-fi set, so he got the driver to offload it into the Landrover and we went back to the desk. Now that we had the documentation, everything flowed smoothly, and the car – and its precious cargo – was at last released, much to the relief of all of us.

That was the first of my brushes with the authorities, but there were several more. Sometimes it seemed as though officialdom was deliberately trying to show its resentment at being on an island occupied by Britain, so it did as much as it could, when dealing with individual Britons, to make things difficult for them.

Another brush with officialdom was over the insurance of the car, which had to be done by a Maltese company, so as I was recently insured with a company called "Eagle Star", which was not acceptable, I had to take out Maltese insurance on the spot. I therefore applied for, and got, a refund of most of my premium from Eagle Star. However, once more what appeared to be a disaster at the time eventually worked to my advantage, when Eagle Star went bankrupt later in the year. "Those upstairs" certainly know what they are doing.

I suffered an example of police corruption many months later. One day, in the middle of the afternoon, an army friend and I had finished work and were enjoying a drink in a waterside café on the road home, when there was an enormous crash outside. We ran out to see what had happened, and found that one of the local horse-drawn taxi-carriages had been driven, at speed, into the back of my car, causing a fair bit of damage. I duly got all the details, made a claim on my insurance company, and thought no more of the matter.

A fortnight later, I was called into the local police station, and told that I was being prosecuted for a number of imaginary crimes which I had supposedly committed, in connection with the incident. The police sergeant read out the list of charges, all of which were totally false, and some of which were even self-contradictory. I was charged with driving without due care and attention, driving backwards on a main public road, deliberately driving into an animal, being parked illegally on a main road, and several others. I protested vehemently, and pointed out that if I was sitting in a café at the time, and had witnesses, I couldn't have been driving at all, but nothing was to any avail. I was definitely going to be prosecuted. However, the police officer told me that if I signed a confession, which would be sent to the insurance company, saying that I was completely at fault, the insurance company would buy the taxi driver a new horse and a new carriage, and all the charges against me would be dropped. It was an insurance scam, aided and abetted by the local police, who presumably would be suitable rewarded.

My next two years were not particularly happy ones, though they were certainly momentous, and one of the most important of all events concerned a disastrous decision we made about Robert. He was quite a chubby little lad, and suffered greatly from the heat and very high humidity in Malta, as I did. (The heat was the one thing about Malta which Eleanor loved, but I hated it.) Robert suffered so much that when my mother-in-law, (Nanny,) came over for a holiday we allowed her to take him back with her to England, reasoning that it would be to his advantage. It was – disastrously so, as it later proved – because he was doted on by his grandparents and by all the many uncles and aunts in the family for the next 18 months, but then, when we came back, he found that he was once more only one of a family of four children. I don't know if he ever really got over the shock, or the resentment it caused.

Another major change was the deterioration of relations between Eleanor and me. The cost of living in Malta was below that in the UK, so there was no tax-free LOA added onto basic wages, and we had no duty-free shop to cushion the cost of purchases either, so we suddenly found that we were relatively poor, compared to our life in France. However, I was still smoking and drinking heavily, and life for Eleanor wasn't good. It got so bad that on one occasion she would have left me, and taken the children with her, if she could have done, but being imprisoned on an island with no disposable cash meant that she was stuck with the situation for the remainder of my posting.

But there was an even greater complication for her: "another home, another child" and our next child was born in "M'tarfa Military Hospital" in March 1961. We had given up on the hope of having a daughter, after three boys, but to our amazement the baby was a girl. We called her "Eleanor", of course, but I was so overjoyed that we gave her a second name of "Désirée – the girl we desired". Today she lives in Perth, in Australia, and has an enormous Dancing School, aptly named "Désirée Dance Academy".

However, the major result of my two years on Malta was in my spiritual evolution, and my almost complete abandonment of the Christian faith. It all had to do with the Maltese Catholic Church. The church hierarchy considered (correctly) that their church was senior in age to the Church of Rome, as St Paul was ship-wrecked on the island on his way to Rome, and converted the islanders to Christianity. So when there was a big international meeting of the Catholic hierarchy in the Vatican in 1962, they considered that they were doing the Pope a personal favour by *allowing* the Archbishop of Malta to attend.

Strangely, though, religious dogma got mixed up with some very outlandish ideas about "the Devil", and these led to weird customs. One of these concerned the clock towers on churches. Only one of the four faces was ever a true clock: the remainder were painted times – and the belief was that if the Devil passed by, he would read one of the painted faces, and see that it wasn't yet time for Mass, so would go on his way and leave the church in peace. (No-one ever queried what would happen if the Devil happened to pass by at the time of Mass, and looked at the correct face.)

Another weird belief was that the Devil was afraid of big bangs, so all fireworks on the island which involved bangs were controlled by the church, and used solely for religious purposes, to frighten the Devil. I once witnessed a procession out of, and back into, the cathedral at Floriana, which was opposite the camp where I was stationed. The procession went out, and came back again, but found the doors of the cathedral closed. So they turned away again, took a few steps, and then turned round, to find that the doors had been flung wide open. Everyone then *ran* into the cathedral, to the accompaniment of a barrage of fireworks. Then once they were inside the doors were closed again.

When I asked what all that had been in aid of, I was told in all seriousness, by a Maltese colleague, that when the Devil saw the procession, he tagged on at the end of it, to try to get into the cathedral and interrupt the service; then, when he saw everyone reach the closed doors, and start to walk away again, he became confused. Finally, when everyone rushed into the cathedral and closed the doors behind them, he had been so frightened by the banging that he hadn't been able to take advantage of the moment.

All of this was far from the Church of England Christianity, in which I had been brought up, but there was far worse to come, and this concerned the sexual ethics of many of the priests. In one case, a priest sexually assaulted a Royal Navy sailor on a bus, and he took offence at the priest's attentions, and hit him. When, inevitably, the sailor was prosecuted, and gave his evidence, the prosecutor said that what he had claimed about the priest could not possibly be true, "as the priest is not on the register of known homosexuals." This was many decades before the question of sexual abuse by the clergy became an issue in the Catholic Church.

However, there was another custom which was so disgusting that it was hard to believe that it existed, but it did, and I saw evidence of it. I know that this story will be rubbished, and hotly disputed by the Catholic hierarchy, but I will tell it exactly as it happened. One day, in the middle of summer, I was being driven through one of the outskirts of Valetta, the capital of Malta, when I saw a furled umbrella hanging on a doorknob. Intrigued by this, I asked my Maltese driver what it meant, and was told that when a young couple married, and the bride hadn't become pregnant within the first year of marriage, the local priest would visit the house to give her "sexual instruction"; to show that he was there, he would hang his umbrella on the doorknob, and while that was hanging there no–one – not even the husband – would dare to go into the house.

However, for me the final straw was the way that the church dominated the life of every one of the local Maltese people – and it concerned their attitude towards fireworks. I said that no-one but church authorities were allowed to buy bangers, and in every parish there was an annual "Festa", which was the feast of the local patron saint. The height of the celebrations was at night, when there would be a firework display, nothing but bangers, and in order to finance this display, the local priest would collect money every week throughout the year from all the local parishioners, many of whom were very poor indeed.

So in the "Festa" season, there would be a different display every week, and over time it became a "badge of honour" of the local parishes to see which one could put on the best display. The last year that I was there, 1962, the declared winner was the tiny village of Lija, who, in the space of about 20 minutes, exploded £10,000-worth of bangers. (In today's terms, that would represent about £50,000, at a time when the average Maltese family income was only about £5 a week.)

This was so far from my interpretation of Christian morality that I turned against Christianity, and – arguably I suppose – "threw out the baby with the bathwater" by rejecting it completely. But of course, by cutting off my roots, I now entered into a state of "nothingness", not knowing what to believe, or how to make sense of an increasingly senseless world. In spiritual terms, I entered into "the dark night of the soul" – but fortunately it didn't last too long.

However, things were happening far away from Malta which would bring my Army life to an abrupt end, and start my civilian career. This was the background: The R.A.E.C. had a long tradition of having most of its instructors as Senior Ranks, with a scattering of officers in mainly administrative posts to do overall organisation. However, the education services of the other Services, the Royal Navy and Royal Air Force, had all-officer systems, and someone in a high Army position decided it would be a good idea to change the whole of the RAEC. So every senior rank in the Corps was given three options, either take a commission, or transfer to another Corps or take redundancy. Well, as far as I was concerned, the first was definitely out – I still remembered with horror "Eaton Hall" – and all that the transfers could offer was a reduction of a couple of ranks (an unthinkable idea after years in a Sergeants' Mess) to go into either the Royal Military Police or the Royal Army Pay Corps, so I chose redundancy, and was made redundant for the first of the three times in my life.

Eleanor and the children were sent home by air, but I had to get the car back, so I drove it through Italy and France, and then back home. Now everything was dramatically different: instead of being in a comfortable large flat, we had to stay with Eleanor's parents in their tiny 2-bedroomed house, and things became very fraught. This is when I saw the folly of my ways in France, and bitterly regretted not having started to buy a house on a mortgage.

At first, I arrogantly expected to be able to demand a council house, as I had "done my bit for my country", but I found out that we would be at the back of a long queue, so we were forced into buying a house, in a nice area of Wolverhampton, for the princely sum of £3,700. Back in the good old days in France, that would have represented merely 18-months of wages, but now things were different, and so were finances. I was about to have to face the rigours of civilian life, which was a massive shock to my psychological health.

Chapter Six:
Introduction To Spiritualism

Before I go on, let me give you some idea of what the transition from service life means to any serviceman or woman, and particularly meant to me. When you are in the Forces, you are part of a huge family, and that is constantly emphasised in several subtle ways. For instance, after the first few years, you are likely to get posted to a new unit, but strange to say, you will rarely feel totally isolated there. Almost inevitably you will meet someone whom you have known before, or find that you both have mutual friends or you will both have been to the same unit at one time or other. All of this will develop the sense of "togetherness" that you feel, and this is enhanced by the fact that everything that you need is provided by the service. In the Army, for instance, the postal service was provided by the Royal Engineers, as was the handling of all movements, including the movements of families. When Eleanor came home from Malta, she didn't need to do anything but clean the flat: a team of engineers came in and did all the packing for her. (When we had first gone to France, five years before, we had one crate and a pram; coming back from Malta, our possessions had grown to nineteen crates and a pram.) Not only that, everything was transported free, and delivered to the door back in England. Other things which were provided for both personnel and their families were medical, educational, social, sporting and recreational facilities – in fact, everything that anyone might wish for – and all was free, which it certainly isn't in civilian life. So to suddenly be deprived of all that back-up, and to have to start making one's own decisions – and paying for them – came as a massive shock.

Chapters in a Spiritual Life

So did I make a mistake in coming out of the Army? Should I have conquered my irrational fear of doing a conversion course to become an officer? Things would have definitely been totally different in my life; I would have almost certainly remained as a teacher, and wouldn't have had all the various experiences – and traumas – that I had in the harsher life of a civilian, or the unforgiving life of industry and commerce. But would I have been happier, or – more importantly – become more spiritually advanced?

This is where sometimes old age is a blessing, as it gives us the one thing so often lacking in our earlier years – time for reflection. (Many lonely old people would complain that they have *far too much* time for reflection, but that is a totally different matter). So now, looking back over the years, I can see that there were no mistakes made; in fact, I have come to the conclusion that it is *never* possible to make a mistake in life at all. Whatever we do has consequences, and if those consequences are "bad" (in human terms,) we can learn from them and – faced with similar situations in the future – avoid making the same "mistake" again. However, if the result of our action is that we have learnt a lesson, it is difficult to accept that the original action was a mistake at all.

My father had many wise sayings which have stuck with me over the years: one was, "The biggest fool in life is the one who pays twice for the same experience." Yet thinking about that now, I realise that if you "pay twice" by making the same "mistake" again, then you obviously didn't learn the lesson the first time, and so needed the second reminder.

So we are all products of all the actions which we have done in the past, and looking back over our life, we can see that everything has brought us to NOW, to this present moment; and if we are *now* able to look at our past life clearly and dispassionately, we have made great spiritual progress towards understanding why we are in this life at all.

However, depending where we are on our spiritual path, we need not wait until the end of life to have this amazing revelation, we can have it at any time. We can help it along by avoiding looking back and saying, "If only I had done *that* at *that* time, what would my life have been like now"? Such thoughts lead on to useless day-dreaming. If we can say, "What have I learned from what I did, and its consequences, which have brought me to where I am now?" then we can start to mentally "close off" the past, and move forward into our new future.

When I got back to the UK, in September 1962, I reported straight away to my depot, Wilton Hall, in Beaconsfield, to find it in total chaos, receiving hundreds of senior ranks from postings all over the world. They were so overwhelmed that I was told to just go home, and stay there until they contacted me to tell me what to do next; so I went home, and for the next six months led a sort of "twilight life" in which everything was unreal. I was still paid my Army wage weekly, but couldn't really make any plans for the future until the Army had discharged me.

However, sitting doing nothing all day wasn't in my character (and still isn't), so after Christmas, when I was still without any official news, I went along to the local school and got a temporary job as a Maths teacher.

This is when I got my next psychological shock. In the Army, discipline was never a problem; for a start I was usually, if not always, senior in rank to my pupils, and secondly they all *wanted* to learn – in fact, in many cases they *needed* to learn – so they were always attentive. However, in a civilian school there was always a core of pupils who had no interest in learning at all, and in many cases found lessons tolerable only by creating as much disturbance as possible, so I now found myself having to deal with indiscipline, for which my RAEC teacher training had never equipped me. So my stay at that school lasted only one term.

However, at the end of the term, in March 1963, I was recalled to Wilton Park to be formally discharged, and so started my civilian life proper.

During the next five years I had three jobs, mostly based in London. One was working as a systems analyst for an international computer firm, a job for which I was totally unequipped mentally. We parted company after two years, to our mutual relief. The next was as an Education and Training manager in a motor insurance company, which was actually being run as a massive scam by an international crook. I was made redundant for my second time after a year, when the company collapsed. Finally, I was employed as a Computer Education

Manager, in a large international construction company, a household name, and that job lasted a further two years, until I eventually got a job back in the Midlands as a Training Officer with a new Industrial Training Board. However, as this book is about my personal spiritual journey, I will mention my work only where appropriate.

My introduction to Spiritualism was once again connected to Auntie Margaret, who had given me my first amazing message back in 1956. (As far as I am concerned, Auntie Margaret was my first "guru" – spiritual teacher – as she introduced me to Spiritualism.)

At the end of 1962, after my return from Malta, she was to come into my life again, but this time with lasting results. By then I was as close as I would ever be to an atheist after my time in Malta; I was certainly an agnostic, a sceptic who needed religion to be proved before it would be acceptable, and was completely disillusioned with Christianity, which had been my basic faith for the past 28 years of my life. One day, when Auntie Margaret was visiting Nanny, her sister, we got into a discussion of Spiritualism. I said that as far as I was concerned it was complete hocus-pocus, and for only the gullible and weak-minded, whereas I was a highly intelligent and mature man, with two professional qualifications in Law and teaching. However, she asked if I had ever been to a Spiritualist service, and when I indignantly said "No.", as I was a rational intelligent being, she invited me to come to one of her services, which were held in a local community centre weekly. I agreed to go, more in order to humour her than out of any real willingness, and duly went along on the appointed evening.

It didn't look much like a church when I went in, just a small room with a table at one end and about twenty chairs arranged in rows, on which were sat a dozen or so women. Auntie Margaret was sitting at the table with a man she introduced as Albert Taylor, a minister from Birmingham, so I sat straight at the back, behind two large ladies, where I could observe everything which went on without being directly involved – or so I thought.

There was little difference between the service and what I was used to in the Christian church – prayers, hymns and an address – until the end, when the minister began to give messages.

Introduction to Spiritualism

He went to the first lady, and started describing someone who was with her. I looked all round, but couldn't see anyone remotely resembling the person whom he was describing, but then he went on to tell her what this person wanted to say to her, before passing on to someone else.

The same thing happened three or four times, and each time, however hard I looked, I couldn't see anyone like the person described, so eventually I came to the conclusion that he was just a kindly old man, well past his prime, who was hallucinating. However, now I was to get a shock, as he said, "I want to come to that young man at the back." I cowered behind the ladies, but he said, "Give me your voice." One of the ladies turned round and said, "He's talking to you; say Hello". So I did.

I will always remember his first words to me: "You have a great work to do for Spiritualism" – which didn't mean anything at all to me then. He went on to describe two people whom he saw with me. I couldn't see either of them, nor could I recognise them as people whom I knew, so eventually Auntie Margaret said to him, "He's new." And he gave up. However, his final words to me were, "Always remember what I have told you tonight: you have a great work to do for Spiritualism."

After the service, I talked to Auntie Margaret and asked her what all that rubbish was about, and she freaked me out when she said that he had been talking to *dead* people, who wanted to contact their loved ones. I was horrified, particularly as I recognised who the two people he had seen with me were – dead relatives. However, I strenuously denied that it was possible for the dead to contact us, and vowed that I would prove that it was all a big fraud.

So started my journey of exploration: a journey which has lasted for 57 years, and is still continuing. No matter how much I have learnt, I have found that there is always more and more to learn.

As I was based in London for the next five years, I had plenty of opportunities to study Spiritualism. There were many churches available, some of which had libraries, and I attended demonstrations at the Spiritualist Association of Great Britain headquarters in Belgrave Square fairly often. I also did a ten-week course on "Introduction to Healing," run by one of the "great names" of Spiritualism, Ursula Roberts. So by the time that I eventually went back to live at home permanently, and work in Birmingham, I had not only forgotten my vow to prove Spiritualism was all a sham, I was completely hooked.

However, before that happened, there were two events which had a great effect on me. During my last job, with the construction company, I had been sent to Bristol on a three-month' assignment, and one evening went to a local Spiritualist church. There was something said during the address which puzzled me, so I went and saw the president after the service to ask for clarification. She said, "Oh, you should have been here last week; Mr .... was the medium, and he is an expert on that." I asked for his phone number, rang him up, and arranged to go and see him.

He didn't seem at all surprised that a perfect stranger should come to see him; in fact, it seemed that he almost expected it. We sat for an hour, and in that time he not only answered all my questions, but gave me so much additional information that it re-orientated my philosophy into a totally new direction. I never met him again, and by now I have completely forgotten his name, but it showed me, for the first time, the truth of the Spiritualist maxim, "When the pupil is ready, the master will appear". This happened a further twice in my life, and now, as I am in the run-up to my final years, I have met my fifth, and last, "guru".

However, the other event was more fundamental, and has affected me far more deeply throughout my life, and that was my introduction to Astrology.

Some people will be horrified at the thought of "Astrology" being mentioned in a spiritual context, but I have studied it, and am convinced that it fits into the overall scheme of Reality, although I accept that scientifically the basic mathematics seem to deny its validity. However, I have read that about a century ago, when the new science of Quantum Physics was being developed in Germany by Max Planck and his colleagues, the "old school" of German scientists ridiculed it, calling it "Knaben-physie", (Little boys' Physics.) At that time, all were steeped in the traditional Isaac Newton laws of Science, and the new ideas conflicted dramatically with those. Yet today Quantum Physics and Quantum Mathematics have overtaken the traditional Newtonian physics, which reigned supreme for more than 300 years. Perhaps one day the same thing will happen to scientific thought about Astrology.

To my mind, if something which *appears* to work goes against the accepted rules, then by all means, try to disprove it. However, if it obstinately refuses to be disproved, then surely there must come a time when it is reasonable to start to query the accepted rules. I wonder how many scientists who ridicule Astrology, based on the phenomenon of the precession of the equinoxes, have actually *studied* the subject with a view to finding out whether or not it works in practice. If they did, I am sure that they would soon find material to make them query their initial scepticism. But now let me tell you how I got into it.

While I was on my Bristol assignment, I used to go home to Wolverhampton every Friday by train, and return on Monday morning. That early morning train stopped at all stations, and the journey took so long that the only way to retain one's sanity was to read. At that time Wolverhampton station had only a tiny kiosk which served as a bookshop, and one day I found that I had read everything which was remotely of interest to me except one book, an Oxford University Press book entitled "Teach yourself Astrology". So reluctantly I bought it, and read it on the way down to Bristol.

I became vaguely interested, and decided to try it out, to see if it worked. The book said if I wanted to draw up a chart for a person, I had to buy an Ephemeris – a booklet showing the positions of the sun, moon and all the planets, for the year of the person's birth; so I chose 1958, the year that Robert was born, and bought the 1958 Ephemeris that week.

I carried out the calculations exactly as instructed in the book, not really knowing what I was doing or what they meant, and after about an hour's work I had drawn up my first ever horoscope chart. Then I had to interpret it. In the book there were some sample interpretations of the various possible positions of planets, and their "aspects", (links to each other,) so I wrote these down, and then read out what I had written. I was staggered: I was reading Robert's character. Then at the weekend, when I read the interpretations out to Eleanor, and asked her who they referred to, she said, "Robert, of course." – And was just as amazed as I had been to find out how I had arrived at them.

From that time on, Astrology has been part of my spiritual philosophy, and certainly it can explain much that is hidden in the character of each of us. In my case, for instance, there is one particular configuration which warns that I will have great potential, but never quite manage to achieve that potential, or – in other words – will "promise much and deliver little" – and that is true to the letter; so many times in my life I have had the opportunity to do great things, but for one reason or another – very often, laziness – have failed to achieve what was possible.

Looking back to my first message from Mr. Taylor, of how I have "a great work" to do for Spiritualism, it hasn't happened yet, and time is now running short for it to ever happen, but I am still hoping against hope that one day it will come true.

(Just in case you think that I am being totally negative here, I will accept that I have done a certain amount of good in my life, and have helped a lot of people to better their own lives, but I haven't done anything which might be called "*a great work*". However, at my advanced age I can now dedicate the rest of my life completely to the service of Spirit, which I have never been able to do before, so perhaps that will make a difference.)

Going back to Astrology, I continued to study it, and became quite proficient at drawing up charts. Then, much later in life, when I was doing "Life Counselling", I developed a technique in which I started every consultation by drawing up a horoscope and showing the client how it had worked out so far, and brought him to their present position. That then helped them to open up and talk to me frankly about their problems, which in turn helped me to help them.

So now, having completely re-indoctrinated myself during those five years, I was ready to go back home and resume normal family life at last.

Chapter Seven:
Spiritualism At Home

As I have said previously, one of the main spiritual beliefs which I have is that everything happens to us for the right reason – for our spiritual evolution. But not only do things happen as they should, they happen at the right time – and here was another example of this in action.

At the start of 1967, things were getting a bit fraught between Eleanor and me, and it wasn't really very surprising. I was away for most of the week, coming home only on Friday nights and leaving early on Monday mornings, but Eleanor had the whole weight of family responsibility on her shoulders for the rest of the time. We had had another daughter three years before, so there were now five children, ranging in ages from 3 to 10, and although the family finances were slightly easier, as I had a very good job in London, she was getting psychologically frazzled, and it was time for me to come home.

Then suddenly, out of the blue, a suitable job appeared. New Industrial Training Boards were being set up, and nationally there was a huge need for Training Officers. I saw an advert for places in the Midlands region of the Road Transport Industry Training Board, centred on Birmingham, and I applied for one and was accepted right away, as at least on paper I was a perfect candidate. There was however, one major snag – the salary. At that time, I was on very good money in London – in fact, the princely sum of £2,200 per annum, which today seems like mere pocket money, but fifty years ago was quite substantial. However, the salary offered in Birmingham was only £1,600 per annum, almost a third less, but there was a company car which came with the job. So I sat down with Eleanor, discussed the pros and cons, and eventually we decided that the advantages of taking the offer outweighed the disadvantages, so in December of that year I started my new job.

The reaction of the children was cautious; as they saw me only at the weekend. I had become a sort of "avenging angel", who judged how well (or badly) they had behaved during the week, and dished out rewards, punishments and pocket-money accordingly. However, the reaction of Nicola, the 3-year-old, was the most amusing. During the week, in my absence, the children were allowed to sleep in turn with their mother, so Nicola said that I could come back permanently only if I took my turn to sleep with Eleanor like the rest of them had to.

Things were now considerably easier for both Eleanor and me, and we settled into a normal sort of family life. The needs of the children were growing, but there were two of us to share the burden (not to mention two cars for running children round in the evenings). Eleanor was able to get a part-time teaching job in a local school, which eased family finances considerably, and although there were family crises from time to time, (often concerning the children,) we coped quite well with them.

There were, however, three major events which influenced both of us for the rest of our lives together. The first happened soon after I came back home permanently. One day, I found out that Willenhall, the town where I was brought up and where my parents still lived, was "twinned" with a French town called Drancy, in the suburbs of Paris, and I went along to one of their meetings one night. They were planning an exchange visit of footballers, and I offered my services to go with the team as an interpreter. Not surprisingly, I was welcomed with open arms, and that started a very profitable association which lasted for more than twenty years. We used to take teenage children over to Drancy, where they were lodged with their French "twins" for a fortnight, and then come back with them, the French children, and their escorts, to return the hospitality.

As an aside here, because of our current mania with "political correctness", "health and safety", and our fear of "the compensation culture", fewer and fewer teachers are prepared to take children on school expeditions, or even run "out of hours clubs"; there are also strict guidelines about the ratio between the number of adults and the number of children on trips, which is – I believe – about 1:6. However, this is what happened on one of our exchanges. There were 52 children, and supposedly three adults, Eleanor, another lady and myself, but at the last minute the other lady dropped out, so we had to devise a plan quickly to control the movements from one place to another of such a crowd.

The ages of the children were from 12 to 16, so we chose seven of the senior children to become "group leaders", and allocated all the others to their respective groups. Then, whenever all the children were together and we needed to do a head count, all we had to do was shout, "Get in your groups.", and the group leaders would gather their members together within a minute or so and report back. It worked like a charm.

There was one very spiritual lesson which I got out of this exercise, which stayed with me for a long time. One of the children in the group was Chris, the "terror of the school", who was now in his final year, by some miracle. (No-one knew how he had avoided being expelled at several times in his school career.) We had been warned by his teachers that he was "bad news", so we could expect trouble from him, and would have to keep an eye on him, to stop him leading others astray.

When I discussed Chris with Eleanor, she came up with a cunning plan: we would make him a group leader, and for the first time in his life give him some real authority. So on the final night before we left, when I was briefing the group leaders, I called Chris aside and explained to him that I was expecting problems with some of the children, so I was going to appoint him as group leader of a particularly difficult group, as I was sure he could handle them.

I don't think that he believed me at first; no-one had ever put him in charge of anything before, let alone a group of people, but when he realised we weren't kidding him, he rose to the challenge magnificently, and during the whole of that fortnight coped so well that he was always the first group leader to report his group as all present. However, that wasn't all; although he had never shown the slightest interest in French in class, he found that he actually had an affinity with the language, and soon managed to carry on conversations with French children unaided. In fact, by the end of that fortnight he had almost become an unofficial interpreter, as children – some far more intelligent than him – were going to him to ask him to help *them* talk to *their* twins.

The spiritual lesson which I learnt from this is that people will often react to you according to how they perceive that *you* judge *them*. (This is, of course, what most child psychologists tell us: treat children with love and affection, and you will get far more out of them than if you treat them harshly.) So in my life I have always tried to see the best in people, and treat them fairly. I haven't always been a good judge of character, of course, and sometimes I have been "taken for a ride" by people I have trusted – but I still use the same strategy when meeting strangers, although few now come into my life.

The second major event concerned my mother-in-law, "Nanny"; she had been widowed several years before, and lived alone in a flat, but it had been obvious for a long time that without someone else to cook for she wasn't feeding herself properly, so we took the momentous decision to move her in as part of our family. We had just moved to a bigger house, so space wasn't a problem, but I don't think that Eleanor had fully understood the old saying that "two women in one kitchen doesn't work". However, it did mean that there was someone there all day to look after the children, (our last child, Penny, had been born two years previously,) and in fact Nanny stayed with us until the end of Eleanor's life – 23 years in all.

As an aside here, I should mention Penny's arrival, which came as a complete shock to both of us. We thought that we had finished having children, and things were rather tight financially, so the prospect of yet another child was little short of a disaster. However, when she arrived she was a delightful little bundle of joy for us, and soon became a great favourite of her many aunts and uncles as well.

However, now something drastic had to be done. Six children, all ages up to thirteen, was a real challenge, so we had to make sure there would be no more. There wasn't the slightest chance of me ever becoming celibate, so one of us had to be sterilised. We discussed the matter, and I realised that an operation for Eleanor would be a very major undertaking, and that left only one option – me – so I decided to "have the snip".

It was an operation that was very new, not yet available on the NHS, and in fact the surgeon who did it admitted that he had done only one previously, which didn't inspire me with a lot of confidence. In order to be accepted, we had to undergo a series of interviews, in which we were warned by everyone that it would mean the end of producing children – and no-one really believed us when we said that that was *exactly* what we did want. However finally, after all the talk, I had the operation. Little did I know that this would eventually give me my greatest lesson in relationships.

I had always been a very highly-sexed person throughout my life. Although a late starter – I was initiated by an older woman at the ripe old age of nineteen, which would probably be seen as *ancient* by modern teenagers – once I started I was like the proverbial rabbit, and regrettably even after getting married I wasn't always a faithful husband, until we moved to France, after which I calmed down a bit,

However, now I was in a completely different ball-game. Only those men who have had a vasectomy can understand the devastating after-effects of it. First, there is a dramatic reduction in the physical pleasure of having intercourse, and that original level of pleasure can never be restored, but of far greater importance are the drastic psychological side-effects.

It is said that when a woman has a mastectomy, she feels diminished as a woman, and I could now understand that, for not only did I feel less virile *physically*, I felt less *masculine* as well. Also, it didn't help that I was coming into a time in my life when – astrologically – I was moving towards the dreaded "mid-life crisis", and I needed a lot of reassurance and building up of my self-esteem. So now, unusually for me, I felt totally vulnerable.

Then into my life came a much younger woman who, strange to relate, *fancied* me, and wasn't afraid to show it. I suppose that flattered my male "ego", something which hadn't happened for a long time Things developed very rapidly, and we had a "one-night-stand", which was totally disastrous; but then a kindly Fate (or "those upstairs" – my spiritual advisors) intervened and she went out of my life just as quickly as she had come into it.

Eleanor never mentioned it, although she must have known about it. Possibly she accepted it as her personal Karma, possibly she was just glad that it hadn't had time to develop into a full-blown affair – I will never know. What I *do* know is that afterwards I was so bitterly ashamed of myself that I vowed never to do anything so stupid again – and I didn't, even though there were several opportunities later in life.

So this taught me a massive spiritual lesson about relationships, and the difference between love and physical/sexual attraction. The latter normally doesn't last very long – even a highly sexual relationship will become stale in time – whereas mutual love can withstand all the knocks that life can ever produce. There may be many reasons why a loving relationship goes through a bad patch, but reasons are never *excuses* to go off and have a sexual fling with someone else. It is far better, when faced with difficulties, to try to work through them together, as if one can do so one strengthens the original bond of love. This proved to be the case with Eleanor and me, as I will explain later.

The other major event was, of course, my full immersion into Spiritualism. We lived in one of the outskirts of Wolverhampton, but this was next to the town where Eleanor had been brought up – Bilston – and where Nanny still lived, so I started going to the local Spiritualist church there. I say "church", but in fact it was very far from the grand churches which I had become used to in London; it was just a small, dilapidated, prefabricated building on an area of waste land just in front of the local railway station, not very imposing at all. Its biggest asset was to prove to be the fact that it had a fairly large car park. I attended there for a few months, and then something momentous happened.

There had for some time been plans to join the main road from Wolverhampton to Birmingham with the M6, north of Wolverhampton, but nobody thought that it would ever happen. However, one day the plans were passed, and the actual route that the road would take was confirmed. It cut through the middle of Bilston, and as luck would have it, through the land on which the Spiritualist church was. So the church had to go, and legal negotiations started to determine the amount of compensation which would be paid.

In the end, because of the large area of land the church stood on, we came out of it very well indeed. Not only did the council award us a plot of land in a quiet area on the other side of town, but they made a cash offer which would allow us to build our own new church on it. The offer was accepted, and it was agreed that we wouldn't have to vacate the old church until the new one was built, as site clearance for the new road wouldn't begin for more than a year.

So work started on our new church immediately. These were heady days for us; at last we were going to have a decent building, "fit for purpose", and everyone was very excited. We started a voluntary offering scheme, in which we each promised a sum of money towards the cost of the final building, and in my rash over-enthusiasm I offered to pay for the ceiling of the main hall. (I have always followed the precept, "Do something in haste and repent at leisure.")

This proved to be the case once again, when many months down the line, after the shell of the building had been put up and it had started to be furbished internally, I was asked for the money for the ceiling. "How much is it?" I asked – and was told £200. I was horrified: this represented six week's wages at that time, when things were not very easy at home. To say that Eleanor was "not a happy bunny" at the news would be a dramatic understatement.

Eventually, either at the end of 1968 or, more likely, in spring 1969, we were in our new church, and revelling in the experience. I started to sit in circle for development, and also joined the healing group as a trainee. I learnt two major lessons in that healing group, two incidents which I still remember vividly after all these years.

The first concerned a lady who had a severely disabled daughter. I never met the daughter, but I learned that she was an adult, mentally and physically disabled, and in need of constant care. One evening I was giving the lady healing, when I was told (psychically) "Tell her she doesn't know how lucky she is." There was no way that I could say that, so I mentally said, "No, I can't."

The order came once more, more emphatically, and I still refused. Finally, I was told that if I didn't do as I had been told, my inspirer would leave me. I still refused, and suddenly all the power drained away, and I was left just standing there, with my hands on the lady's head, feeling very foolish – almost, "Why on earth am I standing here and doing this?" It was such an uncomfortable feeling, that eventually I said to her, "I have just been told to tell you that you don't know how lucky you are", and the lady smiled and said, "Do you know, I was thinking that only this morning."

That taught me a great lesson – which is that our inspirers know far more than we do, and whatever our spiritual gift is, we should always exercise it exactly as we are impressed to. It applies particularly, of course, to platform mediums, many of whom will try to modify the messages they get to make them more acceptable to the listener, but often, in doing so, they change the character of the communicator so that he is no longer recognisable. That is totally wrong. Even if the communicator comes through swearing, and the actual words are not acceptable in a service, the medium should point out that the language used is not acceptable, but it means... and let the listener decide what the actual words were for himself.

The other incident was far more dramatic, and even quite frightening at the time. We held an open healing evening every Tuesday, when there were several healers present and any member of the public could walk in off the street and ask for healing. One night a lady was *carried* in by her relatives. Her body was horribly deformed and twisted, as though she was cowering away from something hideous. We were told that three years before she had walked into a neighbour's house when the neighbour and a group of her friends were playing with a Ouija board. Some entity had come in through the board, and latched onto her, even though she wasn't part of the group, but just standing watching. Since then, she had spent time in a psychiatric hospital, having drug therapy, electro-therapy and other treatments, but nothing could change the condition. The family had brought her to us, as a last resort, to see what we could do.

The seven healers there surrounded her and started to direct healing to her, and for a time seemed to be having some success, but the lady was still saying, "It's still there." Probably meaning that "it" was waiting for us to stop so that it could re-possess her. So our president took the golden cross and chain from round his neck and put it on her. There was an immediate reaction. I had never heard the "scream of the banshee" until that night, nor do I ever want to hear it again, but this blood-curdling shriek came from her throat, and she shot off the chair, as stiff as a board, along the floor. We were all transfixed for about a minute, not knowing what to do, until suddenly the lady sat upright and said, "Can I have a cup of tea, please?" She was healed.

That incident taught me the danger of using Ouija boards, or similar devices like planchettes. There is no danger if the people using them are spiritually aware, and can create the right atmosphere for them to be used safely (and can of course protect themselves and everyone else in the process.) The problem is that very often people use them who are not spiritual, and who are just doing it for a bit of fun. If they attract some entity which they can't control, they have only themselves to blame for the results. The way that I like to explain it is that you wouldn't go to bed at night and leave your front door open, for fear someone might come in and harm you. By playing with Ouija boards, you are doing the psychic equivalent of just that.

Having said that, and in the interest of complete fairness, I have to say that in the very early days, Eleanor and I often sat with two friends and used a Ouija board, but we always protected ourselves before and after its use. We received messages for a couple of years or so, and then one evening, we were told, "You no longer have a need of this." That was that. We never got anything else at all, but by that time we were ready to go onto more direct methods of communication, although I was the only one who actually did.

The main medium at that little church was Pat Handley, a lovely spiritual lady, and she was also a very powerful healer. One night she gave healing to a lady who had a large lump on her neck – probably goitre, or something similar. Pat stayed for about ten minutes with her hands on the lump, and when she took them away, the lump had vanished. That was the only time I ever saw a healing miracle happen.

Pat also ran the development circle, which I joined. It wasn't completely new to me, as I had sat in an open circle at other churches, but now, doing it on a regular basis, I made rapid progress. I soon found out that I had little, if any, talent as far as clairvoyance was concerned – I never 'saw" anything – but I did "hear" things. That is the only way to describe what happened, but the "hearing" wasn't in any way physical, it was just that words and ideas came into my mind.

I now know that this is technically called "clairaudience" – literally "clear-hearing". At first I thought that it was just my imagination playing tricks on me, but Pat encouraged me to "give off" – put into words – what I had heard, so I did. I was told that this was called "channelling", and was a spiritual gift, so I welcomed it with enthusiasm. In time, I began to "feel" the character of the spiritual being that was channelling through me, a very meek and humble person who never gave his name, but said that he was "The potter". He stayed with me for several years, and then was replaced by another being, a Chinaman called "Chang", who stayed with me for many more years.

There are two different kinds of channelling, one of which is known as "full trance", and the other as "light trance", or "overshadowing". Full trance is where the spiritual inspirer takes over the body and mind of the medium completely, so that the medium knows nothing at all of what is happening, but light trance is where the medium knows what is being said, but doesn't have any control over it. My channelling was of the latter kind; the only way that I can describe what I felt was that I seemed to be standing behind myself, listening to what was being said, and occasionally saying to myself, "That's an interesting idea: I had never thought of it like that."

It was a happy and harmonious congregation in that little church, and after about ten years I was asked if I would take on the position of vice-chairman, which I accepted. However, soon after that, there was an incident which brought to an end that happy association.

For those who are not Spiritualists, I should explain that there are different streams of belief, just as there are in mainstream religions. In Spiritualism there are two main schools of thought, those who follow a traditional Christian philosophy and those who don't. In established churches, the title of the church is enough to say what the congregation believe; they are either part of the "Greater World" movement (Christian Spiritualists) or the Spiritualist National Union, (non-Christian.) But in our little church, which was not affiliated to either movement, we were strictly neutral, and perfectly happy to remain that way. Some of the small congregation believed one thing, others the other, but religious theology was never discussed. However, one very dominant old lady, Mrs. Parsons, (we called her "Ma" Parsons) was a definite Christian.

One evening, in one of our regular circles, my inspirer Chang was channelling through me and – as Chang was a Buddhist monk – must have said something that upset Ma Parsons, because she stood up and interrupted, saying, "That is absolute rubbish. There is no true knowledge, except that which comes through the belief in Jesus Christ."Then she sat down again. That cut my link with Chang immediately, and everyone was shocked. Not only was it a complete lack of respect ever to break into whatever was being said, but it could, in certain circumstances, be actually harmful to the medium. As a result of that incident my inspirers told me to leave that church, and never again be involved with the running of any church. They told me that I had to become a "free-lance", who would be taught directly by them. So that was what happened, and for a long period of time I had little contact with organised Spiritualism at all.

Chapter Eight:
Last Days In The Midlands

So for the next few years, little happened on the spiritual front. I was now totally immersed in the business of being a full-time father, and Eleanor had gone back to work as a teacher. In time she would switch from teaching to go into Youth Work, in which she often had to visit youth clubs at night, so I was definitely now a "hands-on" father. On one occasion, late in Eleanor's career, when she had become the senior youth tutor in the local authority, she had to go away to run a residential weekend course, and as Nanny wasn't available, I had to do the cooking. I hadn't the slightest idea what to do. I had rarely had to cook for myself, let alone cook for six hungry children, so I devised a "cunning plan".

On the Friday night I told them that I used to be a cowboy, and I was going to make them the sort of stew that cowboys eat, and I went to the store cupboard and got a few tins of varied foods out, opened them all up, put them in a big pan, and created this new concoction. The children, who were ravenously hungry, wolfed it down. They were less keen when it was served up again for Saturday lunch and decidedly reluctant to eat it for Sunday lunch as well. So when Eleanor came back, later in the afternoon, she was positively overwhelmed by the loving way in which they all greeted her, but I never told her the reason why. These days, all the children are grown up, and some are grandparents, but when I ask them about their main memory of childhood, they all answer, "Cowboy stew."

We bought a small private hotel, which gave us plenty of space, and this was a couple of hundred yards from a Church of England church, so the children started to go there to the youth club, and Penny joined the choir. I was invited to go along to the

Last Days in the Midlands

Men's Bible Study group, which I did reluctantly, as it wasn't quite my thing, but all went well for the first few weeks. However, then came disaster: we were studying the journey of the Israelites to the Promised Land, and came to the section where they besieged a city, took it and slaughtered all the inhabitants, men, women and children. When we discussed this, the prevailing opinion was that they did the right thing, as the citizens didn't believe in the "true God".

This was far too much for me to stomach, so at the end, when the rest of the group had gone home, I spoke to the vicar and expressed my disgust that Christians could even *show* such bigotry, which was totally contrary to the message of love preached by the Master Jesus. I expounded at length my own (Spiritualist) philosophy, and the vicar was kind enough to say that it was the clearest exposition of religious philosophy that he had ever heard, but we decided that there was no point in me attending any more meetings, as our views were so different.

This incident had a strange repercussion many years later, when my youngest son, David, had become an indoctrinated Born-Again-Christian. His church was at that time deeply into asking for forgiveness for past wrongs, and he must have met the current vicar of our old local church, and told him about the incident. Out of the blue I received a letter asking for my forgiveness for the harm that had been done to me all those years before, because of the unsympathetic way the matter had been handled. I hastened to reply and to point out that there was no need to apologise, as no harm had been done; I had had a frank exchange of views with the vicar, and I certainly hadn't been hurt in any way by his "unsympathetic attitude".

This incident made me start to think about the whole subject of forgiveness, so this is an appropriate time for me to explain my own feelings about the matter.

The greatest spiritual writer of the 20th century, Louise Hay, says that bearing a grudge for things that have happened in the past is like carrying a rucksack full of heavy stones on your back. This does you no good whatsoever and you would be far better to get rid of the stones, or even the whole rucksack, and go on your journey a lot lighter.

I agree with her completely and, in my mind-set, remembering past grudges and causing yourself pain is totally self-defeating, and just means that you haven't suffered enough, and need to be hurt a bit more. So in my philosophy, forgiving has nothing at all to do with releasing *them* from a past bond, but everything to do with releasing *yourself*. Therefore the sooner you do it, the sooner you will feel better.

At a more advanced spiritual level, if you believe in the action of Karma, as I do, then you will know that whatever someone has done to hurt you in the past will inevitably be done to them in the future, ("What goes round, comes round",) so that sooner or later they will "get their come-uppance", and nothing that you or they can do will stop that; so if you are looking at the matter from a vengeance point of view, you *will* be avenged, at an appropriate time.

It is a very good spiritual exercise, from time to time, to go back over your life and see if you can remember anyone who has hurt you in any way. Forgive them, and then – just to make sure that you have done a good job – think about them again the following week, and see if you still feel animosity; if so, forgive them again, and imagine in doing so that you are getting rid of another one of your life's problems.

I am going to jump ahead many years now, and to round off this topic of forgiveness tell you what the ultimate spiritual philosophy is. Each of us has a mission, to learn every possible thing about the human condition, and a good way of understanding that is to visualise that, before you came into incarnation this time. You yourself had a huge tick-sheet in front of you. On that tick-sheet are all the human experiences you will ever have to undergo, which will teach you the lessons which you will need in order to understand what being human is. Some of those experiences are already ticked off, as you have had them in previous lives, but now you are faced with choosing some that you haven't done.

At this point in time, every experience is just that – an experience – and you have no concept of what might be called "good" experiences or "bad" experiences, they are all just experiences. Now, as a "for-instance", just imagine that you choose the experience of being bullied. You have no idea what this consists of, but you are told that in order to have this experience, you will need to find someone who agrees to bully you. So you cast around, find someone who hasn't yet ticked off "Be a bully", and you agree that you will both meet in your joint life at an appropriate time. You do meet, and have the experience, with more or less harrowing results. Looking back afterwards, later in life, what are you going to think about your bully?

Well, in 99 cases out of 100, people will say how much they hate him, and wish them all sorts of harm, but you are an enlightened spiritual person, aren't you, a really "old soul", so you know much better than that. You know that it was all arranged before you both came into incarnation, and it was a contract between you. The other person fulfilled his part of the contract, which has enabled you to cross off the "Be bullied" experience on your tick-sheet, which means that you won't have it again in the future; so now, what you *could* do (I wonder if you *will*), is not only to *forgive* him, but to *thank* him for what he has done.

This is a very advanced concept, and very few people will ever understand it, (and even fewer accept it,) but I am sure that you, dear reader, are one of those few. In fact, it ties in exactly with the words of the Master Jesus himself, when he talks about "turning the other cheek". Think about it.

Just a bit more while we are talking about forgiveness: how do you forgive anyone? What do you do, if you ever *do* forgive people? Do you just think of them, say a quick, "I forgive you", and then move on, or is it a more reasoned and serious approach? If you are serious about forgiving someone for a past hurt, and releasing them from your life, then it is worth spending some time to carry out a little ritual to do it. Most of the recommended ways involve some sort of symbolic cutting of the ties which bind you to the other person, and I will tell you of the two most common ones:

Close your eyes and imagine that you have an empty rowing boat on a slow-moving river. The boat is moored, by being tied with a rope to a stake in the bank. Put the person whom you want to forgive in the boat, then, from your heart chakra, (the psychic centre in the middle of your breastbone,) imagine a rose-pink ray coming out, and enveloping the person. Rose-pink is the spiritual colour of love, and you are going to release the person's ties to you in love, so that there are no possible negative energies created.

Keep sending out the love, and watch the ray grow broader, stronger and more vibrant, until the person is completely surrounded by rose-pink light. Then say, "I bless you with love. I release you, and let you go". Now untie the rope which moors the boat, and see the boat slowly move into the stream and float away. Watch it until it disappears.

The second method is very similar, but instead of a boat, you now have a hot-air balloon, tied to the ground. Place the person in the balloon's basket and carry out the same procedure as with the boat. Finally, when the person is completely surrounded by the rose-pink light, cut, or untie the mooring rope and see the balloon float away into the sky.

I personally use a more complex ritual, which involves standing the person on a sea-shore. I then direct successive waves of the rose-pink ray at him, and say, "I forgive you for what you did which hurt me. I now realise that it was all agreed beforehand, and I thank you for having fulfilled your part of the contract so well. I now bless you with love; I release you and set you free". I then continue to send waves of love to the person, and imagine them as being like the waves of the sea, slowly dissolving a sand-castle, as I see him disappear. I finally stop when there is nothing more left, and the sea-shore is empty.

However, very often someone who is still in your life, possibly a family member, is the person who has hurt you in the past, and here you don't want to release the person, just the memory, so you have to modify the method a little.

This time, close your eyes and imagine that you are looking at a blank screen. Now see the particular incident which hurt you, playing out on the screen. See the person involved looking at you, and mentally say, "I forgive you for doing what you did. I now erase the event from my memory." Once more, send out the rose-pink ray from the heart chakra, and see it completely surround and blank out the scene on the screen. Hold that for a short while, and then allow it to fade, leaving you with a blank screen once more.

Last Days in the Midlands

Over the next ten years little happened in the spiritual sense, but it was a time of massive change in the family. The children all grew up and, with the exception of our "baby", Penny, who was still at the local girls High School, left school and got good jobs. Robert surprised everybody, by showing an incredible practical skill as an apprentice Vehicle Body Repairer; in his final year, he was placed fourth in the all-England skills tests, and was chosen to demonstrate Body Repair skills at the National Apprentice Competition; Elly and David worked in finance, she in a bank – she eventually became a Branch Manager – and he in a finance company; Michael became a Vehicle Parts apprentice, and eventually rose to Branch Parts Manager; and Nicola, who was a receptionist in a local 3-star hotel, eventually became an assistant manager of a five-star hotel. So we had a lot to be proud of.

I personally had a more chequered career. After seven years with the Training Board I was "head-hunted" by a local large garage group as Personnel and Training Manager, but seven years later, when the Motor Trade went into decline, I had to close two branches and eventually make myself redundant, for my third and last time. I reluctantly went into teaching, and taught in two local schools, but was never really happy in either.

By 1985, the five eldest children had all "fled the nest", four on getting married and the other one, Nicola, because she took a job in a four-star hotel in London. So our large family of nine was reduced to four, Eleanor and me, Nanny and Penny, and the stage was set for a massive change of circumstances.

This came when we went on holiday in Devon, to a beautiful farm guest-house on the edge of Exmoor. We had a wonderful time there, and I said to Eleanor when we got back home, "We are going to live in Devon". "Don't be stupid", she replied, "What would you do?" "Teach", I said, and immediately wrote to the largest school in the area we had visited, asking about positions. They had no vacancies, but passed my application on to the local Education Authority, who advertised it. A week later, I got an invite to apply for a job as an assistant French teacher at Chulmleigh, a community college in the area. The week before, their assistant French teacher had been offered a promotion, and there was now a vacancy. Another example of, "When something is right, it happens quickly".

So after Christmas in 1986 I started in my new job, and commuted back home at weekends. From time to time Eleanor spent a weekend down with me and we looked for houses, but had no luck at all. We must have viewed about fifty houses, but not one was suitable; something was wrong, and we couldn't work out what.

(As an aside, here, it wasn't too surprising that we couldn't find anything suitable: I had in mind a Devon "longhouse", a traditional home with a long thatched roof, but Eleanor was more into Georgian-style houses.)

After a few months of fruitless searching, we finally found out what was wrong. I had been taken on and given a two-term temporary contract, and was told that a final Selection Board for the permanent position would be held in June. I had been assured that the permanent job would be mine, but one of the candidates on the final short-list was far better qualified than me, and so she got the job.

Eleanor was absolutely furious, and said that it had all been a mistake to come to Devon in the first place, but the day was saved when, a couple of weeks later, I had a job offer from Great Torrington School, in North Devon, who were looking for someone to teach English, Maths and French, my subjects. Now Great Torrington was many miles from Chulmleigh, so we had to start looking for houses in a completely different area. We went into Bideford, and looked in the windows of a couple of estate agents, and in the second one, there was our house – West Iddlecott, a small farmhouse in the shape of a traditional Devon longhouse, built in about 1480, which had been re-modelled with Georgian windows in the 1800s. We put in an offer, it was accepted, and six weeks later we were in. So we were in exactly the right place, at the right time, for the most wonderful – albeit final – years of our marriage.

Chapter Nine:
Bliss - and a Broken Heart

Things didn't start off too well. It was a particularly wet season, and Eleanor, who was at heart a city girl, used to urban surroundings, didn't take easily to living in a relatively remote farmhouse, with only two neighbours within half a mile, but eventually things settled down a bit, and she accepted her fate. However, one day we were having a row, probably about money, which was never very abundant. She won once more, of course – she always did, and I don't know why I ever argued with her – and as I was always a bad loser, I said in a fit of temper, "Alright then, for the rest of my life I will do *exactly* what you say." "I'll believe that when I see it", she replied, and stormed out of the room. (In Iddlecott there were always rooms you could go to when you wanted to be alone.)

Now a few days before, at the dinner table, Nanny had been talking about a man who fawned over his wife, and she said, "He does too much for her." "No man can ever do *too* much for a woman," I had thought at the time; "I bet I could." I now recalled that incident, and decided to make Nanny "eat her words". So I conceived a plan to kill two birds with one stone. I decided to play the part of the attentive husband, catering to his wife's every need, so I started to ask Eleanor if she wanted anything done around the house, or if she needed help, or what would she like to have errands run. At first she was very suspicious – after all it was a complete turnaround from everything she had known for the previous thirty or more years – but eventually, she started to mellow. However, something strange was happening to me as well.

Many years before, when living in France, I had become quite addicted to the works of Georges Brassens, a French poet-guitarist, and one of his songs was about a man who tries to find religious faith, without success. So he consults a religious friend, who tells him, "Go through the motions of being religious and believing, get down on your knees and pray, and sooner or later you will find that you *do* believe". Well, the same sort of thing happened to me, as though I had started going through the motions of being an attentive husband cynically, with the mind-set of "Is this what you want? Are you happy now?" I was soon doing it for real.

That meant that Eleanor, as she relaxed, started to bask in the attention she was getting. She wasn't getting *more* attention these days, but she was getting *better* attention. In the early days, I had done things for her with an air of dominance, because that was what *I* felt was right, but now I was genuinely doing things to please *her*, and make *her* happy. So gradually, as each of us relaxed into having a real relationship, we slipped back to the love which we had felt for each other in the early years of our marriage.

When things go from bad to worse, we call it a "vicious spiral". I don't know what the opposite term is, for when things go from good to better – possibly a "beneficial spiral" – but whatever it is, we were now in it, and we entered into a period of absolute marital bliss, such as we had never known before. Each of us lived 100% for the other one, and we were never happier than when we were in each other's company – and that continued for several years.

However, regrettably "all good things come to an end", and that end came in 1993, when Eleanor, having fought off two cancers during the previous year, one with chemotherapy and one with radio treatment, was too weak to fight off the last, and passed away. I was in absolute denial about her condition, and even assured her surgeon that she would get better, so I went into complete shock after her passing, and that lasted for more than two years.

I now bitterly regretted what I called my "wasted years", the 31 years of our marriage during which I had not found that bliss of the final seven years, but many years later, sitting in circle in Torquay, Eleanor "came through" and said that she wanted to thank me for all the years that we had had together, for the good years and the bad years... "But most of all for the *bad* years, because that is when I learnt". That cut me up completely at the time, for I knew how bad the bad years had been, but afterwards I realised that those years hadn't really been wasted, they had been experiences which gave *both* of us lessons, which were needed before we could evolve spiritually and experience the final years of marital bliss.

I have said that my spiritual life has been in two halves – and the watershed was Eleanor's passing, as everything can really be neatly slotted into "Before" and "After" compartments. It had to happen for both of us; later, during a home circle, she said that she had known that it was time for her to leave: the only thing she was concerned about was how I would cope. For me it was also the right time, although I could not accept it at that moment. That started me thinking about when the right time for anything is: what decides the timing of events in our life?

This is where knowledge of Astrology comes in useful, for it explains everything. Although no two moments of time are ever the same, nor will they ever be for the rest of the existence of the planet, there are recurrent cycles, where planets cross sensitive points in the natal horoscope of a person, and one of the most powerful of these cycles concerns Saturn. Saturn is known as the great teacher of the zodiac, and gives us what we deserve. He is generally feared, as very few people truly believe that they deserve *anything*, and so Saturn gives them just that – nothing. However, working with the energy of the planet, you can achieve miracles.

Now Saturn takes about 28-29 years to go round the whole zodiac, until he reaches the same position that he was in at the birth of the person. This is called the "first Saturn return" and in the life of everyone, marks a time of change. Sometimes the change is caused by physical events, sometimes emotional or spiritual happenings, but change there will be – and we are forced to face up to new situations, review our life to date, and make decisions for the future. In my personal life, my first Saturn return was when I was made redundant from the Army, and the second – at the age of 59 – was the passing of Eleanor. Both were certainly times of massive change and re-adjustment. (Interestingly enough, I am now in my third, and final, Saturn return, at the age of 85, and faced with totally different circumstances to what I have ever known before.)

As a little exercise, look into your own life, and see what happened when you were at the end of your twenties. Was there a change of life? Note that it need not necessarily mean something negative which happened, it might have been a stroke of good fortune, but if there wasn't anything discernible which happened, you are one of the very few people who can sail through life without upsets.

However, timing isn't all about the time of the Saturn *return*. Half-way through the cycle there is another point, which is a sort of "reflection" of the return, and very often is just as powerful as the return itself. How many relationships have broken up when one partner gets a "mid-life crisis", at round the age of 42 to 43? Once more, look round your own surroundings, and see if you can find examples.

The Saturn return isn't the only cycle that is important in our life. Far better known is the seven-year cycle of the planet Uranus, which gives rise to the infamous 'seven-year-itch". Uranus is a very slow-moving planet, and takes 84 years to go round the zodiac, but every seven years he connects with where he was in the natal chart, and usually brings some sort of change. The most amazing example I have ever seen in my life was a close friend, who, every seven years, broke up a stable relationship by having an extra-marital fling and moving out. I was able to chart this, which happened with absolute regularity, for 42 years, after which I lost touch with her. (I hope that she has now learnt her lesson, as she must be well into her eighties.)

Interestingly, the same Uranus effect touched the life of my beloved second wife, Sybil. After twenty years of marriage, when conditions had deteriorated badly, she decided to split up from her husband, but after long discussions stayed on. Seven years later, the same conditions reappeared, and she once more decided to leave, but eventually didn't. However finally, when the same conditions re-appeared again seven years later she left, and got divorced. (This was long before she met me.)

The Uranus cycle occurs in everyone's life, but it isn't always connected with relationships, nor is it always necessarily harmful.

Bliss - and a Broken Heart

In my life, for instance, with unfailing regularity I have either changed my job, or done another job within the same company, every seven years, and last year was the time of another change. I am now faced with a situation that has never occurred before in my life, so it will be interesting to see how that develops.

I spoke to one of my daughters about this Uranus cycle, and she agreed that it existed, but in her life it had manifested itself in a move to a new house every seven years. So, look at your own life, and see if you can see any sort of seven-year pattern in the past, in any area of life, which might help you to predict when things might change again in the future.

I have spent a little while talking about Astrology, so let me explain why; I have no wish to convert anyone who believes either that it is all hocus-pocus, or that Astrology is incompatible with spirituality. We all have our own philosophy of life, and I honour the beliefs of everyone, regardless of the path they take. However, Astrology has been very important in my life, and although I am no expert I have had enough experience of it to show me that it has *something* to do with the ultimate reality of human life, although I cannot rationalise it, or explain the connection. It has been a long time since I did horoscopes for people regularly, but I still do the occasional one, in connection with counselling, as I shall mention later.

So Eleanor's passing was a time of complete devastation for me, but also it marked the opening of a new era of spiritual developments, and those developments came in thick and fast. One of the first things that I learnt was how to use the powers of spiritual beings, by invoking them (calling on them.) I don't know how I found this out, but it was probably from something which I read, as Eleanor's passing had spurred me to do a lot of spiritual reading again. I learned to invoke archangels: Lord Michael (the Archangel Michael,) lord of the heavenly host, for physical protection, Raphael for healing, Gabriel for spiritual inspiration, but most important of all, Zadkiel, (whose name I didn't previously know.) Zadkiel is the keeper of the violet flame of transmutation, (complete transformation,) and has the power to transmute all negative energies, in any situation, and convert them into Love, the highest form of light. He then releases the Love, for the benefit of the Universe.

Now Zadkiel's energy is extremely powerful, and should really be used only in emergencies, as a sort of spiritual "First Aid treatment", but when I started to use it, soon after Eleanor's passing, I found it so effective that I used it continually, not realising what harm I was doing. In fact, after a while, I used to boast that I could go from the depths of despair to normality in about 20 seconds, if I invoked Zadkiel. However, what I didn't realise was that kindly Nature has provided us with a "release valve" for emotion, through tears, which drain away excess grief, and if one deliberately stops the flow of tears, one builds up a dam wall, behind which the pressure of emotions gradually increases.

Before I continue, let me give you the Zadkiel invocation. To invoke any spiritual being, all that is necessary is to call their name three times, and they are forced to be with you, by spiritual law. So this is what you say:

"Zadkiel, Zadkiel, Zadkiel, I ask you to be with me now. I ask you to surround me with the violet flame of transmutation; I ask you to transmute all negative energies around me into Love, the highest form of Light, and release it for the benefit of the Universe.

I have many stories about how effective – and how quick – the invocation is, but this is probably the most amazing of all of them:

I was contacted late one evening by a lady, who told me that she had just been phoned by a friend, who had driven to a rendezvous, 200 miles away. The friend had had an enormous emotional shock, and intended to commit suicide, so she was ringing up to say "Goodbye". The lady tried to dissuade her, but the friend was adamant, and rang off, then switched her phone off. I was asked if I could help.

The only thing that I could do, without a possibility of speaking to the friend directly, was to invoke Zadkiel, and ask him to surround the friend with the violet flame, in order to lift the negative energies round her – so I did just that.

Early next morning, the lady was once again phoned by the friend. Surprised, she asked where the friend was, and she was told,

"At home". Even more surprised, the lady said, "Well, a few hours ago you were 200 miles away, and determined to commit suicide; what happened"? The friend explained that as soon as she had put her phone down, a feeling of complete peace came over her, so she said to herself, "Oh, well, I had better drive home now" – and she did. Powerful stuff, this Zadkiel invocation.

I was taught the lesson about not suppressing emotion when, about a year after Eleanor's passing, a completely unrelated incident brought tears to my eyes, and once that happened, the dam burst, and I was plunged into the depths of grief. Everyone can understand, and make allowances for, grieving immediately after a passing, but very few people can understand it when it happens a year later. So now, although I use Zadkiel frequently, for myself and for others, when teaching the invocation I am always careful to point out the dangers of relying on it too much, or using it too often in a bereavement situation.

Another thing that happened just after Eleanor's passing was that I was brought into contact with the works of Louise Hay, as explained in her seminal book, "You can heal your life". I shall expand on this a little later, but at the moment let me say that she outlined a philosophy in which all illness and disease starts with a psychic cause, and if it is possible to neutralise the original cause the illness will disappear, in the same way that if you cut the roots from a tree, the tree will die. I bought the book, and immediately went to the end of it, where Louise Hay gives a list of illnesses, and suggests possible psychic causes for each illness, and – chillingly – found out exactly what killed Eleanor. So this is now an appropriate moment for me to speak about Eleanor, my "Wonder-woman"

Chapter Ten: Eleanor – The Wonder-Woman

First of all, let me give you a few facts. Towards the end of her career in the Midlands, Eleanor was the senior Youth tutor in the local authority, organising and teaching the residential courses for senior youth workers which occurred several times a year. She supervised the running of nine youth centres, which involved her working three nights a week, and she started two community associations based in different areas of the borough. She also supervised the running of a third, which was already established. As a side-line, she ran three one-woman businesses. The first was in dressmaking, (she specialised in making wedding dresses;) the second was in catering – she was an expert in making celebration cakes, and made one, for the wedding of David, our third son, which weighed over a hundredweight and consisted of seven tiers, all beautifully decorated in Wedgewood blue and white; while the third was in floristry (she had a floristry diploma.) Oh, and she successfully brought up six children, all of whom have excelled in their diverse careers.

What has all this got to do with Louise Hay? This is where Eleanor's life (and death) taught me a massive spiritual lesson. Looking up the psychic causes of cancer, I found that the chief one was Resentment – and reading that I knew exactly what had killed her. All her life she had bitterly resented her mother, who had brought her up in the grim surroundings of North-East England, where the man of the house was God, the children came next, and the woman was always at the end. So Nanny had brought Eleanor up to believe that she would always be inferior to men, and she was even forced, as a little girl, to clean her elder brother's shoes.

Eleanor - the Wonder-woman

There were many ways in which this showed itself in her upbringing, but possible the most traumatic was the following; when Eleanor was eight, there was a school concert, and she was the first turn, singing a solo. However, Nanny, who got her and her brother ready very late, dressed the brother first, despite Eleanor's protests, so that when they arrived at school, they had missed the start of the concert, and also Eleanor's chance of stardom. The depth of her bitter disappointment – and resentment – was shown fifty-five years later when, on her deathbed just three weeks before she passed, she still remembered the incident.

However, she rebelled against her conditioning, and determined that she would show that she was just as capable of success as a man. (In fact in later life, when asked if she believed that women were the equals of men, she always answered "No." When people expressed surprise that such a successful woman should say that, she always continued, "I am not the *equal* of any man; I am *superior* to *every* man." – and she meant it.)

She had a very hard childhood, with a lot of illness, so that she missed her "11-plus" examination, which would have allowed her to go to a selective grammar school, but for the next two years she worked hard at school to catch up, and at the age of 13 she had another chance to transfer, and passed the exam. Now, of course, she was far behind her classmates, who had been working at an increased pace for the previous two years, but once more she worked hard, and not only caught up but surpassed them all, and eventually became the top scholar and the Head Girl of the school.

She then decided to become a teacher, and went to a Teacher Training college. She wanted to do a full Home Economics course, but was forced to do only a shortened course, because her salary was needed at home, where there were another five children to feed.

So in 1952, she started her first job as a teacher, and was immediately faced with the harsh reality of life as a woman, where she earned just £28 per month, half of what a male teacher earned.

Over the years, she worked very hard, and eventually became acting Head of a large Junior School. Then she decided to change careers, and joined the Youth Service of the Authority, where she found that there was even more discrimination against women.

Once more, she worked hard, and eventually got recognition for her ability, as I stated earlier.

So what spiritual lesson did her life give me? Well, once more, it had to do with Predestination and Freewill, and also tied in with Astrology. An astrological chart is a snapshot of the moment of birth, and when interpreted shows the framework which the person chose before coming into incarnation. It also shows what the conditions of the life will be but, interestingly, it does *not* show how the person will react to those conditions: that is a matter for Freewill. When faced with any situation, there are always two possible ways of looking at it: we can see the glass as "half-full" or as "half-empty" – we have the choice.

There is a spiritual saying which sums this up neatly: "There are no problems in life, only opportunities." If we consider something as a problem, we are likely to feel negative about it, and about the possibility of changing it but if we think of it as an opportunity, then we start to think positively about ways of finding a solution.

In Eleanor's case, the obvious injustice of a male-orientated society might have made her just accept the situation, as most of the girls in that environment would have done, and her life would have been totally different in every respect; but she didn't. She fought against the injustice in the best way possible, by showing that she was just as capable as any man, and eventually she won the day.

However, there is another aspect of Eleanor's story which is a bit more difficult to understand. That is the fact that it was the injustice, focussed through her mother that led to Eleanor's eventual success, and yet it was that same injustice which eventually brought about her death, as it caused the illness which ended her life. So how can one reconcile the fact that the same condition can cause two apparently opposite results, one "good" and one "bad"?

I think that the answer lies in the use of the words "good" and "bad". If we can go back to first principles, and the idea that each of us comes into incarnation with the aim of learning certain lessons, if by the end of our life we have learnt those lessons, then the result cannot be thought of a "bad" at all. However, it can't be thought of as "good" either; it is something that was intended to happen – was *predestined* to happen – and it happened. Our use of the words "good" and "bad" is just a sign that we can't understand the spiritual significance of what has happened.

This applies also, of course, to the timing of death. When we have carried out all the tasks that we came here to do, and have learnt all the lessons, there is no further need for us to stay in this life, and we are *"allowed"* to go home, and this will apply to all of us, regardless of the age we are. Once more, with human understanding, we say that if a person dies young, or what we consider as young, then that is a waste of a life. Not so. They have done what they wanted to do, what they planned to do, and there is no further point in them staying here.

The idea of "an untimely death" comes sharply into focus, of course, when we are faced with the passing of a child, for whatever reason. When this happens, those who knew the child usually speak of him or her as "a little angel", "a delight to everyone", or use some such glowing words, and for a time, certainly until the funeral, there may be a great outpouring of grief. But what could be the spiritual purpose of such an early death? This is something that very few people ever consider – the possibility that an early death can ever have any beneficial consequences.

Yet that early death has in fact pointed us to an eternal truth, that when we come into incarnation, we are a pure spiritual being, and it is only when we are being raised as children that we start to become corrupted by the negative beliefs of others, and usually those of adults. Take the case of racism, for instance. Two young children, from different backgrounds or with different racial/ national/ religious characteristics, will always play happily together until – or unless – the differences are pointed out to them, and they start to become indoctrinated. Teach children love and respect for all others from the start, and that is how they will turn out to be as adults.

Let me add something here which very few people – even Spiritualists – realise. Children are only children in *human* terms. In reality, they are already glorious *adult* spiritual beings, as we all are, and as such are just as capable of making pre-life decisions as the rest of us. So if they have decided to come into life for a specific purpose, which can be accomplished in a few years only, who are we to say that they were wrong. Meditating on this might make it a little easier to understand the meaning behind the "untimely death" of a child.

Now, to return to where we started this chapter, and to my beloved Eleanor, I owe an enormous debt of gratitude to her for how she shaped my spiritual education, before and after her passing. She very literally taught me how to love. I had never had the parental example of marital harmony, so I thought that marriages always had to be backgrounds for confrontation, and that is what my attitude was in the early days of our marriage; it was only in those final glorious years that I learnt what marital love really meant, and it didn't end with her passing.

She still continued to express that love for me long afterwards, and foretold my meeting with Sybil, and our future together. She was also seen by one of my grandchildren, who was psychic, between Sybil and me on the day of our wedding, with her arms round both of us, giving us her blessing. Not only that, but she has always added her own love for both of us to the love that we have for each other, so we have been doubly blessed.

One small "aside" here: I decided that mourners shouldn't waste money on flowers at her funeral, but donate to a fund, the proceeds of which would go to the local hospital, so on her coffin there were only eight red roses, one each from Nanny, the six children, and myself. So now, every time that she "comes through" to me, she brings a red rose. The other evening, in a reading, she brought two red roses, one for Sybil and one for me.

It was just over two years after her departure that I met Sybil, and a mere seventeen months after that that we got married, and there were some people who thought that it was far too early for another relationship, and showed disrespect for Eleanor, but obviously she didn't see it like that. So perhaps now is a good time to have a look at the whole subject of second relationships.

First of all, all relationships are expressions of love. These days, that is a dangerous thing to say, as the word "love" itself has been so debased that it is often used to signify sexual relations, which it certainly doesn't. Love is not sex, and sex isn't love. Each can exist without the other, and they should never be confused. In certain circumstances, sex can be a way of demonstrating love for someone, but in others it can't. For instance, one can love an animal, a child, one's parents or a member of one's own family, but sex with any of them would be completely taboo.

However, for our purposes, let us imagine that we have two people in some sort of close and intimate partnership, marital or otherwise, and one of them dies. Some time later, the survivor meets another person, and starts a second relationship. What are the spiritual implications of this?

Well, the question was asked of the Master Jesus, who answered it in the most direct way possible – "In the kingdom of Heaven, there is no marriage, nor the giving of marriage". So that is the spiritual answer, plain and simple.

The problem is that we do not really understand the meaning of "love". On Earth, the love between two people is understood as being an exclusive relationship, and this, once more, is because we see it in a sexual context. Sex with the partner is normal, sex outside the relationship is not, and is destructive. However, if we remove the sexual aspect from relationships, then things become much clearer. We can have many dear friends, and love each one just as much as any of the others. We can love both parents equally, or many brothers, sisters, or children equally. We can love several pets equally, and so on.

In none of those examples is there any form of exclusion. Of course, exclusion *can* come into relationships. Many people have friends, but when you get "best friends", then possibly the thought of cutting out others from the relationship can eventually lead to jealousy, and the break-up of relationships.

So let me now focus on my two relationships, with Eleanor and with Sybil. Which one is/ was best, and which person do I love more now?

Well, the question itself is totally ridiculous, as it is like trying to compare chalk and cheese. Each has its values – you wouldn't want to try to eat chalk or to write on a blackboard with cheese, so trying to compare them would be stupid. Let us start with my love for Eleanor: I still love her today just as much as the day when she left this planet and in fact writing of her today brought memories – and tears – back to me. However, what we had together, and the loving energy we shared, is now fixed for eternity, and can never be altered in any way. It is still there, vibrant and alive, and can be re-visited at any time, but can never be added to, detracted from, or changed in any way. There is an old saying, "Memory is the only happiness", and the memory of that love between Eleanor and myself still brings me a great deal of happiness.

The love which I feel for Sybil is totally different; it is neither "better" nor "worse", but different. We have been together for only 24 years, so are hardly out of the honeymoon stage yet, but our love is continually evolving, changing, plumbing new depths, and so is like a kaleidoscope, continually showing new faces as conditions around us change. Every day brings new possibilities of expressing that love, and adding to its vibrancy.

As I said, Eleanor taught me how to love and so Sybil and I started on a completely different footing to what Eleanor and I did; in fact, we have still never had a proper row. Of course, we irritate each other from time to time, (I irritate her with some of my habits more than she irritates me with hers,) but none of that detracts from the love that we have for each other. (She did once throw a vacuum cleaner at me, but I just told her not to be such a daft old bat, and that calmed her down. At least, I think it did: she didn't say much for the next couple of days or so.)

Finally, when we all make our own transition, and get to "the other side of life", we will understand the true meaning of the word "love", as we bask in it, in company with all of those whom we have ever known, without any form of human emotion getting in the way.

Chapter Eleven:
Counselling

My introduction to Louise Hay's work had very profound effects on my future. I read the book thoroughly, and could relate to all that she said, so I decided to try it for myself. I started with simple affirmations, and then went on to more complex ones, and found them all effective. So I decided to start teaching her methods to others. (For anyone who is open to new thoughts on self-improvement, I thoroughly recommend the book.) By that time, I had finished working as a classroom teacher for the Devon LEA, and I was working as a home tutor, visiting boys who were unable to do mainstream education, either because of illness or because they had been permanently excluded from school because of bad behaviour. I was on a hiding to nothing, really, as most of my clients had no interest whatsoever in education in any form, and certainly not in doing any actual studying, but I found that I was able to get through to a few, and help them to try to put their life back on an even keel.

Some of the boys I had to visit were in a Local Authority care home. There were some violent boys in there, but not all: one of my clients, who was quite a gentle soul but who had severe psychological problems, was one of my few successes there. I was supposed to be teaching him Maths, but instead I taught him the elements of Louise Hay's philosophy, and put the idea into his head that he could achieve anything he wanted to do, if he concentrated hard enough on it. I asked him what his greatest wish would be, and he said fervently, "To get out of this place". So we decided on an appropriate affirmation, and he started to use it.

Soon after that, I was moved from that home to go to see other clients, but I met one of the tutors a few months later, and asked him about my former pupils. He told me that the one I was particularly interested in – the one I have just mentioned – changed his behaviour completely, and so impressed the Educational Psychologist on his next routine visit that he recommended that he be moved to another home; so he was moved to a home in a sea-side resort, full of non-violent children, where he had his wish granted, and eventually became a model pupil. Thank you, Louise Hay.

About six months or so after Eleanor's passing; I received another hammer-blow of Fate. Nanny's other daughter, who lived in Scotland, had been angling for a long time to get her to go up and live with them, as she reckoned that I wasn't able to look after her, (Nanny was in her early nineties by then,) so eventually she gave in to the daughter's pleas. My brother-in-law came down to Devon to collect her, and after 23 years of living with me, she finally left.

Now I was really alone, and could thoroughly understand the meaning of loneliness; I had never, in all my life, been completely alone. I had always had people round me, family, friends, Army mates, work colleagues, etc. – but now I was alone in a large ten-roomed farmhouse, which felt as empty as a tomb. In order to find myself something to do, to relieve the utter boredom, I decided to do some voluntary teaching in the evenings. Some years before, in one of my schools, I had worked closely with the Special Needs teacher on a computer project, and with her encouragement I had devised a method of teaching children to read, and particularly a way of fixing letter combinations in their mind. I wrote a book on it, and tried to get it published, but no-one wanted to know; however, I still had all the notes, so I used them to help some of the local children who were having trouble reading. In one or two cases, where the mother was a single-parent, I found that she also had problems, so I started using my new-found skills as a counsellor to good effect.

Over the course of the next few years I taught – or tried to teach – fifty-three boys as a home tutor, and there again I found that many of the mothers who were single-parents had problems. One of these, whom I shall call Ann, although that wasn't her real name, was in a horrendous state when I met her. Her life had been a total mess, from start to finish. She was one of a large family, and her mother had died when she was twelve, so she had had to take on the role of being "mother" for the family. After three years, she had a mental breakdown, and was put into a psychiatric hospital, where she was raped by two of the inmates. When she came out "cured", she got married, only to find that she had really "jumped out of the frying-pan into the fire", as her husband had more psychological problems than she had. She was left a few years later with two young boys to bring up, both of whom got into drugs, and one eventually took an overdose, which killed him. The other one took so much LSD that he became totally psychotic, and unable to attend school, and I was appointed to be his home tutor.

I tried to get him to think of attending college, in order to do some course or other, but he was adamant that he wouldn't be able to stand the course. Seeing the opportunity to do a bit of good work on him, I introduced him to Louise Hay's work, and affirmations, and to becoming more positive. Finally, I asked him to make up an affirmation about college which would start with the words, "I am positive..." He did so, and said the words, so my hopes were raised that I had made a breakthrough, only to be dashed again when he continued, "......that I *can't* go to college".

I still continued seeing him for the next two or three months, until the end of the school year, and of my commitment to him; after each session I spoke to his mother about him, but after a while this led on to her talking about her own problems. When I had first met her I had had a psychic vision of being in a car in the dead of night, without brakes or lights, careering down a hill at an ever-increasing speed. It was a hideous feeling, but it just about described her life at that moment. Things were getting worse rapidly, and she was in dire financial trouble as well, so in order to get some sort of qualifications for herself, she had enrolled on a hairdressing course at a local college, and was now approaching her final exams.

I started to work with Ann, using Louise Hay, and things slowly got better. I helped her financially, taking her shopping weekly and paying the bill, and when she had a last-minute hitch on her college course, in which she needed to do a month's work on a project in a few days in order to get her final certificate, (months before someone had forgotten to tell her of the project which had to be produced,) we worked together over the weekend and she got it submitted just an hour before the deadline.

I grew very fond of her, but there was never any sexual motive; there couldn't be – I was still in deep grief, only a year after Eleanor's passing. However, then there was an incident, a difference of opinion, and she cut herself off from me completely. I had looked on her almost as a father looks on a daughter – she was 25 years younger than me – so I grieved as if I had lost a daughter – and something strange happened. I started to shed tears for my loss, which was absolutely against my normal detached Aquarian character. But now, having started to cry, the dam which I had created through using Zadkiel was shattered, and all those pent-up emotions flooded out unhindered.

Now when any disaster happens in our life, after the initial shock (and possibly grief) we tend to ask questions: what caused it to happen, could it have been avoided, etc., and in doing so we often learn the spiritual lesson which the incident was destined to teach us – and so it happened in this case. I went back to my own natal horoscope to search for clues – and found them. They revolved around Pluto, the smallest of the planets; in fact, it has been now degraded by astronomers to the status of "dwarf planet", as it is so small. However, small though it may be, it is one of the most powerful spiritual influences in any life, and can turn a saint into a sinner, or vice-versa.

Wherever Pluto is in a chart shows the area in which a person will be controlled in early life, and in my chart he was in the area which deals with religion, philosophy, Law, further education and foreign countries and people, and as I said earlier, I had been dominated in every one of those. My mother had forced me into the Christian church, which controlled my religious philosophy for so many years, in further education she had forced me to study Law, which I hated, but on the plus side she had sent me on that school trip to France, and give me a life-long love of the language and country.

Now there are two sides to Pluto, and two ways of dealing with the after-effects of our early experiences of him. Negatively, in adulthood we can either continue to be controlled by other people in that area of life, or we can rebel, doing the exact opposite and controlling others.

When I analysed my life, I saw that I had chosen the latter; I had controlled Eleanor throughout our marriage, with disastrous effects, and had come into the blissful period at the end only after I had given up control to her. I had controlled Ann as well; the control had been mental, emotional and financial – fortunately not sexual, which would have added an extra complication – but eventually she had broken away from that control.

However, if we look at the positive side of Pluto, if one is able to renounce the need to be either controlled or to control others, one can release enormous spiritual power, so this is what I decided to do in the future, which had immense effects on my spiritual development, as I shall show later.

It was not a happy time, but I eventually got through it, and continued my working with excluded boys, and occasionally their mothers, and I actually managed to help people change their life on one or two occasions.

Then I had another spiritual happening – I met my third "guru". I was with my eldest daughter Elly at a service in Barnstaple, where the medium for the night was Ron Buckle, a homeopath from Exeter. At the end of the service, I turned to Elly and said, "What did you think of that address?" "I don't know," she replied, "I didn't understand a word of what he was talking about." I said, "That is the most amazing address I have ever heard. I must go and see that man." So I rang up his practice and booked an appointment to see him.

When I went in, I confessed immediately that I was there under false pretences, as I didn't want a consultation; I wanted him to explain his address the previous Sunday. He didn't seem surprised at all, and for the next hour gave me more and more information, stopping occasionally, to say, "But you know that already" – and I realised that I did. He was reminding me of knowledge which I had forgotten that I had. He opened my mind to other aspects of which I knew nothing at all, of contacts with cosmic forces and entities, and life-forms on other planets. Finally, he gave me a reading list of books which would further my knowledge, which I duly bought and added to my growing library. I saw him only once more before he passed, but that remains another one of my experiences of the saying, "When the pupil is ready the master will appear."

Then something else amazing happened on the spiritual front, something which was destined to change my life for ever. Over the years at Iddlecott I had begun to build up quite a large library of spiritual books, and as I had a lot of time on my hands now I did a lot of reading. I had also started to attend one of the two Spiritualist churches in the area, Barnstaple, about ten miles away, and Bideford, about twelve. On occasion I was asked to take a service, but as I wasn't clairvoyant I had to just give the spiritual address, and rely on an established medium to do the clairvoyance. However, one night there was no medium available, so I did the whole service. My main speaking guide gave the address, and then another guide answered questions from the audience about the address; this formula went down quite well, so I started doing it regularly, whenever I was invited. It was billed as "An evening of philosophy."

However, now there was a series of "co-incidences" which was so stupid that they could only be explained by our old friend "Predestination." There was a medium from Paignton who had been booked for a Sunday evening service in Bideford church, and one of his Paignton friends, Clare, had learnt that he was going. She had once lived in Bideford, and still had friends there, so she decided that she would "kill two birds with one stone", visit the friends and go and support the medium as well. However, the medium went down with the 'flu, so on the Thursday he rang the church secretary and cancelled. They were then in a bit of a fix, and couldn't find a replacement at such short notice, so they rang me and asked if I was available. I was always available – my life was full of empty evenings – so I readily accepted, and that set the scene for the prelude to the rest of my spiritual life.

I went to the church and did my normal thing, with the address and then questions, and afterwards, as I was going out and down to the tea-room, a lady stopped me and asked to speak to me. It was Clare; she said that the address which I had given was the most inspiring one she had ever heard, and asked if I would be prepared to go down to Paignton and ask my inspirer to talk to a group of her friends. I agreed willingly – anything for a change – and a date was set for a fortnight or so later. I went and performed, and that was the start of an association which has now lasted for 25 years.

I started going down to see Clare regularly, every fortnight or so, and met some of her amazing friends. Among them she had a Buddhist monk, a time traveller, a past life regressionist, a psychic artist, several healers and many mediums, so I was gradually introduced to a wider and wider circle of spiritual people, which absolutely blew my mind. Apart from the two churches I mentioned, I had had no contact with spiritual people for many years, and now to be surrounded by them was totally refreshing; but what was most strange was my relationship with Clare.

I felt very close to her, in fact I felt that I *loved* her, yet not in any sort of romantic way – it was much deeper than that. I did ask her why she thought we had come together, but she couldn't give me any logical explanation. However, many years before, when we first moved into Iddlecott, I had had a vision of a plumpish lady with a halo of blonde hair, and I felt that vision somehow *linked* to Clare, although it was not *her*. In fact, I even asked her if she knew anyone of that description, who was widowed after a happy relationship, but she didn't, so I forgot it.

One day we happened to be talking about Astrology, and she said that she had never had a horoscope done, so I offered to do one for her, and on my next visit I interpreted it. One of her friends saw it, and also asked for one, and before I knew it I was starting to do astrological charts again, after a break of 25 years.

I was now getting very close to Clare, and this disturbed me somewhat, as I couldn't quite work out what I was feeling. It wasn't physical attraction, although she was quite an attractive woman, then almost 50 years old. It was only much later that I found out the answer: we had been together in many lives, going back to Ancient Egypt, and in many relationships, including one in which we were married; and in this life she had come to do an important job of work – bring Sybil and me together. I didn't know this at the time, so it is not surprising that I felt confused.

Chapters in a Spiritual Life

In late 1995, Eleanor came to my daughter Penny, through a medium, and forecast that I would be getting into a relationship shortly, and although I hotly denied the possibility, it must have started to condition me for what was to happen a few weeks later. Then it happened. Clare was a very mercurial person, on top of the world one minute and down in the dumps the next, and she hit a real "downer" this time, just before Christmas. So to try to pull her out of it, I suggested that she should throw a party. I said that it needn't cost her anything – she could ask all the guests to bring a "bottle and a plate", which would cover the catering side, and it would mean that I would have the opportunity of meeting some more of her wonderful friends. So she agreed, and a provisional date was fixed for the 15th of December. However, at the time Clare lived at the top of a very steep Close, and there were few parking places in the street, so at the last minute she phoned me and said that the venue was going to be changed, and instead of her house it was going to be at her friend Sybil's house.

She put Sybil on the phone to give me instructions how to get there, and while we were chatting I asked her if she had ever had her horoscope done. She said that she hadn't so I offered to do one for her if she gave me her date, time and place of birth – and the silly woman did. No sooner had I put the phone down, than I went to the computer and put her details in, and produced her horoscope, which told me all about her character. Then, out of curiosity, I did a "compatibility chart", which was a comparison between our two horoscopes, to see what sort of relationship we could possibly have together, and the result was absolutely fascinating; it would be either a complete disaster from Day 1, or it would be one of huge spiritual power, when we were working together. So before I ever met Sybil I knew all about her, and was looking forward to finding out which interpretation would be correct.

I took a bottle of wine along to the party and a big Normandy apple pie which I had baked. That night I was going to stay in Torquay with Sue, one of my counselling clients, so I went and picked her up and we went to the venue. It was a small house, filled with about twenty people, and Clare met us and introduced us to Sybil.

Counselling

The party was a huge success. There was plenty of food and drink, and although many of the people were strangers to each other, everyone was very spiritual, although working in different ways, so we all got on like a house on fire. Sue had a particularly marvellous time; a very vivacious lady, she was in great demand all night, and was never left alone. I had long conversations with Sybil, and found that we were on the same wavelength, which was not surprising; she is a Sun-sign Libran, and I have a Libran ascendant. However, she has a Leo ascendant, and Leo is the organiser, the person who brings people together, and then watches to see how they get on together. Later that night, I saw her doing just that, sitting on a settee in the corner, by herself, just noting how people were relating to each other.

The morning after the party, when I left Sue's flat I realised that I had left the big baking tray on which I had made the apple pie at Sybil's, so I went round to get it. Clare was still there, as she had stayed the night, and she had just predicted that I would return – and ten minutes later there I was. I offered to drop her off home on my way back to North Devon, and she invited me in for a coffee.

We chatted about the party, which had really lifted her spirits, and she asked me what I had thought about Sybil. I replied that I found her very charming, and then I unconsciously slipped into channelling mode, and foresaw a little bit of her future. I told Clare that she would either have two relationships, one after the other, with different men, or she would have two phases of a relationship with the same man, the first temporary, the second permanent. Then Clare asked innocently (Oh, so innocently.) if that man could be me.

I was a bit shocked by the question, but then suddenly everything came into focus. Sybil was the lady in the vision I had seen, (the description fitted perfectly,) she was the one who Eleanor had predicted would come into my life, and as Clare was the link between us, that was the energy I had been feeling which so confused me. That night, I phoned Sybil, and was on the phone for two and a half hours. The next night I phoned again, for three and quarter hours, and by the end of that call we were in a relationship. We had decided that we would have a "trial run" for two or three months, and then, if things hadn't worked out, would part without any hostility or recriminations.

Three months later I took her to Paris, and we stayed with long-term French friends from Twinning days. During that visit, we both went to the Sacré Coeur cathedral and, kneeling in prayer in front of the massive image of the Master Jesus, independently vowed the rest of our lives to the service of Spirit. So by the time we came back, we were in a permanent relationship, and Eleanor's prediction had come true to the letter. "I will bring a lady into your father's life, and by the spring he will know that she is the one."

As an aside here, long before we met, Sybil had visited an international medium, Dorothy Chitty, and asked her if she would ever have another man in her life. Dorothy had replied that there was another man already "waiting in the wings", but he would be the exact opposite of her ex-husband in every way. However, she and her new man would "fit together like two pieces of a jigsaw puzzle." That prediction couldn't have been truer. Sybil's first husband was very neat, tidy and organised, a workaholic, and a brilliant craftsman and I am exactly the opposite; I am quite a scruffy individual, highly disorganised, rather lazy, and with no practical skills whatsoever. However, I am quite a romantic at heart and, having served my apprenticeship with Eleanor, know exactly what love is, and how to show love. Also, although we have totally different characters, Sybil's strengths cover my weaknesses, and vice-versa, so we do "fit together like two pieces of a jigsaw". (Strange to relate, we are also both jigsaw fanatics.)

After a month together, all our friends were saying that we were behaving as though we were an old married couple, and when something is right, that is certainly how it feels. I have never regretted a moment of our life together, and Sybil feels the same.

Chapter Twelve:
Brave New World

Meeting Sybil was the start of my new life. As well as the entry into a deeply fulfilling personal relationship, it was the start of my regeneration into Spiritualism. After the relatively barren time in North Devon, with little spiritual activity, I now found myself immersed in an area where such activity was everywhere. Torbay is now a Unitary Authority, consisting of three small resort towns, Torquay, Paignton and Brixham, but in those days they were still separate, and each one had a lot of weekly Spiritualist activity going on. Apart from the two established churches in Paignton and Brixham, there were several small independent meetings, run by local mediums in halls or private houses. A little further away, there were also churches in Newton Abbot, Teignmouth and Dawlish. So there was always plenty of opportunity to attend services or demonstrations of clairvoyance. I was really spoilt for choice.

However, before I continue, I had better speak about the *sort* of relationship I wanted with Sybil. As I said earlier, the self-analysis which I had done after breaking up with Ann had made me resolve not to dominate in any future relationship, but here we came to a clash of characters. Sybil had been divorced for three years, and – still a fit and healthy woman, with quite a "young" outlook on life – was very lonely. (This is the case with many Librans who live by themselves.) So she was completely ready for another relationship, particularly remembering the predictions which Dorothy Chitty had made. As far as I was concerned – and particularly after Eleanor's prediction – I was also ready for a new relationship, but this time I wanted to give up control, and concentrate on the spiritual side of Pluto.

So I exercised my last bit of control, and over the next year or so manipulated Sybil so that she was forced to take control over her own life, and the major matters in our joint life. This has led us into having a very unusual relationship. From one point of view, we lead almost separate lives, she does her thing and I do mine, and we never question each other, but in all joint matters she is in charge, and she knows that whatever decisions she makes, I will support her 100%. So that fulfils the emotional needs of both of us – we have a very deep companionship, without ever having the constraint of feeling that we are in a "cage", as is the case in some relationships.

It was 64 miles from Iddlecott to Torquay, so I soon started to stay overnight with Sybil, and the occasional night grew to several times a week, until I was spending more time in Torquay than I was back at home. By this time, due to Government changes in the rules for excluding children from school, the supply of potential home pupils was drying up, and eventually it stopped completely, so that although I was technically still employed by the local Educational Authority, they had no work for me. I received only dole money every week, for which I had to sign, so I had to be home for that day and time, but apart from that I was free to stay where I wished.

I enjoyed those early days very much and we often went to services or demonstrations in local churches or centres. It was still much too early for us to get actively involved in running a centre, but the novelty of choice was enough for me at the time. However, it was time for another spiritual revelation.

Once more it was a set of "co-incidences" which brought everything about, once more an example of predestination. One of our friends was going to a conference of "Walk-ins" in Street, Somerset, and as she had no transport we offered to take her there in our campervan. When we got to the venue, we found that there were still places vacant on the course, but no accommodation, so on the spur of the moment we decided to stay and enjoy the weekend. We found a local site to park the campervan, and enrolled. That weekend was a complete eye-opener for me: I had never even heard the term "walk-in" before, so I had no idea what it was all about, but I found that it was possible for someone to leave their life and physical body, but instead of the body disintegrating, as it normally does, for that body to be taken over by a highly spiritual being, who is coming to Earth to do a particular job of work. Such a spiritual being is known as a "walk-in" – and all of the people at that conference were either walk-ins themselves or closely connected to them.

The most well-known walk-in was a woman called Ruth Montgomery, who wrote a book about her own personal experiences, but there have been many others. Strange to relate, I have now recently met another walk-in, who is probably my fifth and final "guru" in this life.

Although we met some amazing people that weekend, and learnt a lot of new things, it had another more lasting effect on me: we met a lady who was to become my fourth "guru", and teach me most of what I know about spiritual energy. She had produced a set of spiritual "vibrational energy" devices, and we used to go to Mind, Body and Spirit exhibitions and market them. I worked with her for about nine years before circumstances intervened and took me away, but I am still in touch with her even now.

However, it was now time for another major event in my life, this time on the emotional front. We came to what I (jokingly) call "Black Friday", February 28th, 1997. It started off normally enough. We were going out to visit Sybil's parents, on a routine Friday visit to spend an hour with them and make sure that they were alright, but just before we left Clare arrived with another friend, Jean. So we told them to have some coffee, and make themselves at home till we got back. On the way to the parents' flat, Sybil asked, "By the way, are you ever going to ask me to marry you?" I was a bit surprised by the question, as the subject of marriage had never been mentioned before. We had slipped into a lovely easy relationship, and I was quite happy to remain that way. I had made a commitment to Sybil, and as far as I was concerned that was that. But I suppose that women don't see things that way, they want formality, a formal commitment, certificates, and things. So I replied, a little surprised, "I suppose so; why do you ask?" Sybil replied, "Well, Clare has a rather nice ring which she wants to sell, and I thought that it would make a good engagement ring." "OK," I said, "I'll have a word with her when we get back." And promptly forgot the matter.

When we returned home after the visit, Clare said, "Well, what did he say?" and Sybil produced the ring from her bag. I should have smelt a rat then, but being a bit thick I didn't, so I had a look at it, agreed that it was quite nice, and settled a price with Clare. However, now things took a more ominous turn. Clare said, "Right, well you'll have to propose now"; and between her and Jean I was almost forced onto my knees to propose, which I eventually did, (and was accepted, of course.) Then the final hammer blow came, as the three women began to discuss possible dates for the wedding. I had no say in it at all: I was stuck in the situation, and before the afternoon was over, the date for the wedding had been set – nine weeks later. Now you see why I call it Black Friday: at the start of the day I was a carefree bachelor, and by the end I was engaged, and had a date fixed for the wedding. (By a strange coincidence the date we got married – 3rd May 1997 – was the fortieth anniversary of Sybil's previous marriage.)

The next realisation was that whatever the good intentions were, we had one big problem: we were broke – and weddings don't come cheap. However, as soon as our friends heard that we were to be married, they all rallied round and provided almost everything. One provided material for all the bridesmaids" dresses, and for the page boys" waistcoats, and Sybil made them all; another did the flowers for free; my daughter Penny, who at the time was managing a holiday camp, got her chef (who lived in Paignton) to take a holiday and cater for the reception; daughter Nicola, by that time Assistant Manager of a 4-star hotel in Sidmouth, booked the owner's personal suite for our first night; another friend, who was a very good amateur photographer, provided the album and photos; another friend made the cake; French friends invited us to stay with them for our honeymoon – and so it went on. We were married in the Spiritualist Church in Paignton, and held the reception for 100 people in the hall at the back of the church.

As an aside here, although there had to be a registrar in attendance to register the wedding, it was Clare who conducted the ceremony. So she introduced us, provided the engagement ring, forced me to propose, helped set the date for the wedding and finally, to make sure that I couldn't wriggle out of it, married us. She has a lot to answer for, that girl.

However, amid all the happiness there was one incident which caused sadness, although it also gave me another spiritual lesson, and provided my final severance with Christianity. As soon as the date of the wedding had been set, I phoned all my children and told them, and invited the grandchildren to be bridesmaids or page boys. But when I spoke to David, my "Born-Again-Christian" son, he asked where the wedding would be held, and I told him. He said, "In that case there is a problem, as my wife and I have vowed to God that we would not put foot in any religious place other than Christian." I was a bit shaken, but he then said, "However, we will come to the reception; where will it be?" I told him, and when he knew it was in the same building he refused once more. I suggested that he asked himself what the Master Jesus would say in the situation, and he said that he would "go away and talk to God" about it. Well he did, and God must have said 'Stuff them.", or words to that effect, as the next week he came back to me and apologised for the fact that the family wouldn't be able to attend, as they had booked a holiday in France for that week. So that is what he did, and what he told his children, who were disappointed at not being bridesmaids.

That was the last straw for me; despite all that I had seen in Malta, because of my early conditioning I still had a tiny gut-feeling that somehow Christianity had a slight moral edge over all other religions; but now I realised that bigotry was bigotry, and Christian fanatics were just as bad as the fanatics of any other religion. He had deliberately caused harm within the family, and bitterly hurt me. This was the one day when I wanted the whole family to welcome Sybil as one of us, and here David was, implying that because she had different religious views she was inferior. It took me some time to get over that hurt but now, following what I said earlier about forgiveness, I can not only forgive him but also thank him for having shown me that Christianity without spirituality is no better than any other religion.

So we at last started married life together. Well, I say "started", but nothing changed from the previous situation where I spent half of my time in Torquay and half in North Devon. Of course, it made me realise that there was no further value in keeping Iddlecott, so I put it on the market; however, when it didn't sell, after a year or so I took it off again. We were still in dire straits financially, but eventually that changed two years later when I got to 65, and could receive my pension. As well as the state pension I had a Teacher's pension, so we were now relatively well off and when I put the house on the market again in 2000, it finally sold for a reasonable price.

This is where I pass on some spiritual advice to all who are changing home. I don't know when I learnt this, or how, but it is a little ritual that I do every time that I leave anywhere and move on. I spoke earlier about releasing individuals, and mentioned some rituals which can be used in forgiveness, but this touches on a far greater subject, the subject of Energy. All of us are beings of energy, and when we react with anyone else we have an exchange of energy. But energy can also be held *within* objects, and in fact one of the spiritual gifts often practised is Psychometry, in which the medium senses the energy *stored* in objects, and by doing so is able to give a reading about the persons who owned them. Now if that is possible with personal objects, how much more is it possible with places. So therefore, if you do not completely cut your link with the energy you have put into the house over the years, you will always have a tie with it, which is often felt as nostalgia. So you need to do a little ritual to cut that link.

What you do, as the last thing before you finally step out of the building, is to go into each room, (including "the smallest room") bless it with love and release it. I personally stand in the room, with arms outstretched and eyes closed, and say, "I bless you with love. I release you, and let you go." When I finally left Iddlecott this was particularly important, as that held the energies of all those wonderful last few years with Eleanor, and I certainly had to make a clean break. So I did that little ritual everywhere, including the barns and outhouses, and then walked away – and I have never since felt the slightest attachment to the place, or even had any urge to go and see it again. It is in the past, nicely wrapped up in my memory, and put away.

So that was the end of an era. The past, and all my links to it, except those with my own family, had now gone, and I could move into the Brave New World of spiritual evolution which beckoned me.

Chapter Thirteen:
Manifestation And
Predestination

When I started to go to see Sybil regularly, I found that she was deeply into Spiritualism. She had joined a local church ten years before, found that she had a gift for healing, had undergone training and was now a very accomplished healer. She had also run several development circles for young clairvoyants and mediums, so when she ran the next one, I was able to join in and experience the delight of sitting in circle once again, after a lapse of twenty years or more. At one time we had the thought of buying a property and setting up a spiritual centre, and in one circle, her inspirers asked her what she would like in it, so she made up a list of requirements.

There would have to be at least five bedrooms and a couple of bathrooms, to cater for overnight visitors, and a big meeting room, where talks could be given, and workshops take place. In addition, one or two smaller rooms, for circles or small discussion groups would be nice, and of course, as catering would be important, a well-equipped kitchen. People would have to travel to get to the centre, so a generous number of parking spaces would be required, and then, for leisure purposes, an outdoor swimming pool. When she had finished, her inspirers said that she had been remarkably modest in her requests, as she could have asked for much more, and they suggested that we should concentrate on what she had specified. I don't think that she thought for a moment that she would ever get her centre – but she did, as you will see later.

Manifestation and Predestination

There was one major event in 2000 which was to alter the lives of all the family, and give me the final proof that Predestination was a factor in the life of each of us, and that concerned Elly, our eldest daughter. Many years previously she had married Howard, a sailor, and he had just finished his 22 years of service and was about to retire. But what would he do in civilian life, and where would they live? The answer came in a very strange way. This is quite a long story, but it shows that there is no such thing as "co-incidence", so it is worth telling.

Many years before, my daughter Nicola had gone to London to work as a receptionist in a four-star hotel. Then, as now, the cost of lodgings there was scandalously high, so the only thing that most people could do was to "house-share", where several people jointly rented a big house, had their own private rooms but shared the amenities, and so that is what Nicola did. She stayed in London for several years, and had a succession of flatmates, of whom many, "by co-incidence" were Australian. She became firm friends with several of these, and when they left to go back to Australia, they all invited her to pay them a visit at some time in the future.

That time came in 1988. There was a scheme in which Australia would welcome young people up to the age of 25, and would allow them to "back-pack" round the country for a year, which was often a "gap-year" in between studies, so when Nicola was 24 she decided to take advantage of the scheme. She contacted all her old Australian friends, (who "by co-incidence" lived in different cities), and arranged to go and visit each of them in turn, in Perth, Adelaide, Melbourne, Sydney, Brisbane and Cairns. So off she went. She came back before the end of the year, for some reason. All that I knew was that I suddenly felt a desperate need for her to be back in the UK, and was glad when she finally arrived home.

Of course, she told wonderful stories about her exploits in Australia, and what a wonderful country it was which so filled Elly and her husband with curiosity, that they decided that one day they would go there for a holiday. So when Howard left the Navy, they did just that. They went out to Perth, and stayed with one of Nicky's friends. On the first day there, they had a remarkable "co-incidence". On the way back from an outing, they pulled into a garage, and saw a young woman polishing the windscreen of the car in front of them. Elly said to Howard, "I know that girl; I used to work with her." "Don't be silly", said he, "You can't have done". "I did", said Elly, and got out of the car to speak to her. "Hello, Sue." she said, to the girl's amazement: it was indeed the same girl. She was in Australia on a "gap-year", and was staying with her uncle and aunt, Harry and Joan. She introduced Elly, who in the future became firm friends of her and Howard.

They fell in love with Australia, and decided to emigrate. It wasn't difficult for them to get residence permits. My beloved Eleanor had been born in Australia, so all the children had an automatic right to citizenship, and Howard was a highly skilled electronics technician, one of the people whom the government there needed, so all went through smoothly, and they emigrated in August 2000. They stayed for the first fortnight with Harry and Joan, who then became their "mentors" and helped them to acclimatise during the first year or so that they were there.

As soon as they got there Elly contacted us and suggested that we should go out and stay with them for a holiday. They were renting a large house in one of the outer suburbs, and she sent me photos of it. In fact, she also sent me the details of her estate agent's website, to show us the kind of houses that there were in Oz. We looked through the list of several hundred houses, to rent or buy, and were amazed at how ridiculously cheap they were, compared to prices in the UK. So on a whim I picked out a large house at random, downloaded it, and showed it to all our friends, to show them Elly's new environment.

I had never had the slightest intention of going to Oz. When I was made redundant from the Army we had been offered the chance to go out to Melbourne, where Eleanor's uncle had a top position in the planning department, but I had scornfully rejected it. Why on earth would I ever want to go to the opposite side of the planet to live? So I wasn't particularly keen to go on a holiday there, but Sybil – far more adventurous than me – eventually persuaded me, and we went in early November, when the temperatures of the Oz summer were really starting to rise.

Manifestation and Predestination

Then Elly had a bright idea; why didn't we buy a property in Oz, as I had a large amount of money available from the sale of Iddlecott, and prices there would only rise rapidly in the future, as the city expanded, so it would prove to be a good investment. I allowed myself to be persuaded, so we went house-hunting. In Oz, they have a system of "Open homes", in which the owners of houses for sale hand the house over to their estate agent for an hour or two, and during that time any prospective buyer can walk in off the street – without an appointment – and view the property.

That first Saturday we must have seen more than half a dozen properties, which was total overload. When we got back, we couldn't remember whether any individual property had been the one with the beautiful portico, or the magnificent built-in bar, or the stunning swimming pool, or other interesting features, so we decided that that wasn't the way that we would find a suitable home.

The next weekend we tried a different approach, and bought the local newspaper on Friday night, which had a few properties advertised. No pictures, just descriptions. So we chose what seemed to be the best of the lot, a couple of 5-bedroomed properties, and made appointments to see them the next day. The first one was nice, but didn't really have any "Wow" factor, but the second – well, as soon as Sybil walked through the front door, she said, "This is mine." It was ridiculously cheap, the equivalent of £90,000, which was only half of what I had got for Iddlecott, so we said that we would have it.

This is where we found out something else amazing. In this country, there is a long period of time between an initial offer and acceptance and the final contract, but not in Oz. 18 hours after we had seen the house, the estate agent came round with a contract, and we signed it – and were committed. The only thing that could then have broken that contract was if the house failed any of the statutory inspections, for termite infestation, subsidence or other major structural faults. These various checks were carried out by experts over the next four weeks, and then, on 25th January 2001 – Australia Day, and the day that my youngest daughter's first child was born – we moved in.

But I have missed out the most amazing fact of all. When we had signed the contract, the estate agent said, "Oh, by the way, I will leave you a copy of the house particulars", and when we saw them we realised that they were the same as the ones which I had downloaded back in the UK, several months previously. It was the same house. If one considered everything which had led up to that result as a series of "co-incidences", it would stretch the imagination beyond statistical limits, so the only conclusion one can come to was that everything was *pre-destined.*

We stayed in Perth for another two months, after which Elly and her family moved into the house as caretakers, and over the next few years it hosted everyone who went out to Oz, either on holiday or in order to emigrate. So eventually, in a strange way, Sybil got her wishes, as the house measured up exactly, word for word, to the centre which she had specified years before; it had five bedrooms and two bathrooms, a very large open-plan family room, with a well-equipped kitchen, a smaller lounge, capable of being divided in two, car parking space for about 15 cars, and a wonderful swimming pool. The only thing which she had not specified was the location, which she had automatically assumed would be in the UK. This taught us a lesson; there is an old saying, "Be careful what you ask for, you might get it." But to that we must now add, "but be precise in all your requests."

Three of the other children followed in quick succession, Robert, Nicola and Penny, so then my family in the UK was severely depleted. David also eventually followed, many years later in 2015, and now the only one left is Michael, my eldest son, but as he is approaching retirement, happily married and settled in his lifestyle, I don't think that there is much chance of him following suit. However, I have the feeling that towards the end of our own life, Sybil and I will emigrate to either Oz or New Zealand, (where the climate is far milder, and more like the UK climate,) so we shall see.

Chapter Fourteen:
Reincarnation

One of the cornerstones of my spiritual philosophy is the belief in Reincarnation. In fact, it is probably truer to say that my whole philosophy is *based* round the concept. Yet what led me to this belief in the first place? Again, it was a "coincidence", or rather synchronicity, once more proving that everything happens at the right time. My study of Astrology had showed me that the moment of birth sets the framework for our whole life, and this seemed totally unfair. Why was one person destined to be born rich, another poor; or one healthy, another sick; or one intelligent, another stupid. How could there be any "divine justice" in such a system?

Then one day, when browsing through the volumes for sale in a used-book shop, I was attracted to a book called "There is a river", which was the life story of an amazing man called Edgar Cayce, an American seer. I read the book, which completely "blew my mind", and introduced the concept of Reincarnation to me, and subconsciously it took root. For those of you who are avid readers, I can thoroughly recommend this book, which I am sure you will find as amazing as I did.

However, learning the theory of it and actually experiencing it are two different things, and I have vivid memories of the times when it was confirmed as being valid, through a series of what I call "flashbacks". These are spontaneous regressions back to an earlier life, 'seeing' – and reliving – episodes in that life, and often linking them to people who were connected to me in this present life. The first of these took place soon after I came back home to work in the Midlands in 1967.

Eleanor and I had taken the children on holiday to France, and were in the South-west, an area which we hadn't visited previously. We were going to visit Carcassonne, an ancient mediaeval city which had been completely rebuilt in the 19th century, and brought back to its former glory. No tourist vehicles were allowed in the city, so there was a huge car-park just outside the walls. I drove into the car-park, got out of the car, and saw the walls for the first time.

I froze. I was absolutely terrified, and couldn't move. I saw myself as a soldier, part of a force which was besieging the city, and I was climbing up a very long ladder from the dry moat outside the walls. Then, when I was almost at the top, someone threw something searingly hot down on my head, and I fell into the moat – and oblivion. The memory was so vivid, and so horrifying, that I must have stood there for at least two minutes, transfixed, and terrifying Eleanor and the children, who didn't know what was happening. But then I came back to reality, and explained what I had seen. I don't think that Eleanor understood me, or believed what I had said – she was just glad that I was back to normality again.

That was the first time that anything like that had happened, but in time it proved to be only the first of many such incidents, some of which were quite as dramatic. All in all, I think that I had ten such flashbacks, to different lives and different periods of history, and interestingly enough they linked with eight people whom I knew at the time in this present life. However, I would have to wait almost forty years before an event happened which proved the trigger of the flood of revelations which came in.

Once more, this came about as a result of a series of "co-incidences". One of my counselling clients was dyslexic, and as well as helping her overcome some of her negative life conditioning I had also helped her conquer her dyslexia. Then, in 2003, she emigrated to Australia. She came into contact with a dyslexia organisation, and found out that they "might be" recruiting a dyslexia teacher, so she suggested that I might be a suitable candidate. This is where facts got a bit confused with wishes, and the distinctions got a bit blurred, as she contacted me and led me to believe that there *was* a job waiting for me if I went out there; so I made an application to the Australian government for a work visa, and was granted a provisional one for a year, provided that the job was forthcoming. In the end, it wasn't; either the organisation had changed its mind or it had all been a misunderstanding in the first place, but there was definitely no job at all. I did get some temporary work as a volunteer teacher, with an organisation called "Read Write", helping adults who had literacy or numeracy difficulties, so I stayed in the country for almost my full year, but then I had to come back.

However, the big event which happened during that time, which proved to be a massive leap forward in my spiritual evolution, was my introduction into Australian aboriginal life. Once more, a series of "co-incidences", which were so complicated that I won't detail them, but which introduced me to a lady who had worked with local aboriginals for so long that she was now considered as an honorary elder of the local aboriginal tribe. I will call her "Olive", although that was not her real name.

Let me break off here to explain that Australia has had a very chequered history in relations with the aboriginal population. Whenever British explorers found new lands, and there was an existing civilisation, they integrated with it, and usually eventually smothered it, and assimilated the new country into the British Empire. However, when there was no existing civilisation, the land was declared "Terra Nullius" (Land of no-one"), and it was colonised immediately, regardless of the wishes or needs of the existing inhabitants. This is what happened in Australia: as the local inhabitants had no central organisation, but were split up into hundreds of small tribes, the land was declared "Terra Nullius", and therefore "up for grabs", and as the original settlements grew, more and more aboriginals saw their traditional tribal lands occupied by the new invaders. This led to great antagonism, but dissension was crushed, very often brutally, as it was believed that the existing inhabitants were a sub-human race, and as such had a status little more than animals.

Today, more than 200 years after the first British settlers landed in Botany Bay, New South Wales, to found a penal colony for offenders in Britain, aboriginals form a very large underclass in Australia, and tend to have worse jobs, worse housing and worse prospects than the rest of the population. Dispossessed from their tribal lands, cut off from their traditional way of life, many have succumbed to the twin evils of modern society, drink and drugs, and are seen as the "dregs of society", but fortunately not all. There is an "upper-class" of aboriginal life which has retained the traditional teachings, and the traditional knowledge of their ancestors, and today more and more Australians are recognising the values they have, and are being drawn to the ancient wisdom. So at last, in the present society, the tide is turning to acknowledge all the disastrous policies of previous generations, and right some of the many wrongs. I was fortunate in making contact with this "upper-class" aboriginal society, with an introduction into the local tribe in Perth, the "Nyoongars".

I have said earlier that I worked for more than nine years with my fourth "guru" on a series of spiritual devices which generated vibrational energy, and I eventually arranged for her to donate two full sets of these devices to two senior aboriginals, both elders in aboriginal society, one of whom was the 'senior aboriginal lady" of all the aboriginals in Australia. So through them I came into contact with many members of the local aboriginal tribe, which eventually led me to receiving two "initiations" as a member of the tribe. The first was done by Olive, who as an honorary elder was allowed to carry out initiations.

A date and time was set for the initiation, which was done in Olive's home. It was a very long procedure, lasting almost two hours, which I shall abridge, so that only the main points are emphasised. It started with having one of my feet massaged, using kangaroo oil, and then with "ochre". Ochre is a kind of earth, ground down into fine powder, and there are three kinds of ochre, red, yellow and black, all of which are used for different grades of initiation. I started off with the lowest grade, which I think was the red ochre. I have no idea what minerals are contained in the ochre, but they certainly had very dramatic effects.

The ochre was massaged into my foot, on top of the kangaroo oil, which was just a carrier, and both were eventually absorbed into the skin, leaving the foot completely dry. Then the same was done to the other foot. I was then told to close my eyes, and relax, and after about ten minutes I was asked what I could see. I thought that this was a daft question, as I had my eyes closed, but suddenly I realised that I *could* see something. As I concentrated, I saw that I was looking at a camp-fire, and behind the camp fire were a group of aboriginal people. In the middle of the group was a small lady – at least, very small in height but enormously big round the waist. In fact, she looked as though she was bigger round the waist than she was in height. Then Olive started to ask me questions. What was I seeing? Who were the people? Where was I? And strange to relate, I found that I was able to answer her. These people were all my relatives, and the small lady in the middle, who radiated pure love, was my grandmother, and the grandmother of the whole tribe.

After that, Olive told me to leave that scene, and look again. What did I see this time? So I did, and saw another picture, this time a view of a landscape, with strange shapes of hills and woods. I duly passed on what I had seen, and was told to go to another scene – and so it went on. By the end of the session I was confidently describing not only scenes, but also people in those scenes, and giving names of places, individuals, tribes, and so on: an amazing experience for someone who had never had given any clairvoyance at all.

Some time later there was a validation of this experience, which happened when I was visiting the senior aboriginal lady. When I went into the house, she was busy talking to a visitor, so she told me to go through to the veranda at the back, which I did. There, in the doorway, I saw a small lady, and as soon as I saw her I knew that we had met. I said to her, "I know you – we must have met". "I don't think so", she replied. Then suddenly I remembered: she was the lady whom I had seen in the middle of the group by the camp-fire. "You were the grandmother". I said, and she immediately went back into that previous life, smiled, and said, "Yes, I was." What an amazing "co-incidence". In this life she was the seeress of the local tribe, what might be called the "medicine woman" in other cultures, and she was routinely consulted on all important matters to do with tribal affairs.

The post of seeress was hereditary, handed down from mother to daughter, and I met both her daughter, the 'seeress-in-waiting" and her granddaughter, who at the age of 11 already had great psychic ability, during my time in Oz. There was one interesting incident when I first met the daughter: she immediately said to me, "You are a wizard". I couldn't understand what she was talking about, but she explained that in aboriginal folk-lore there were people who had great spiritual powers, who were known as "wizards" – and one could always tell a wizard by the fact that he had a certain bone formation on his forehead, a letter "V" – and I have that very formation in my forehead. So my "code-name" for my email address is now, "Ralph thewizardofoz".

My other initiation was just as dramatic, possibly even more so. I was visiting the senior aboriginal lady one day, when a group of foreigners were there, six or seven in all, as well as half a dozen aboriginals. I can't remember all of the nationalities, but there were definitely Canadians and a couple of Norwegians among them. I don't know what governs when initiations are scheduled, but during the afternoon, the senior aboriginal lady suddenly said to me, "It's time for your next initiation." and it started. I was well aware of the procedure now, and everything seemed to flow very smoothly. I was taken back to previous lives, in different parts of the country and with different tribes, and I described the areas I was seeing, gave names, and often what I was seeing was validated by one or other of the aboriginals who were there, who was familiar with the area. I was now much more fluent with the new power, and so the names of people, tribes or places, most of which were totally unknown to me, were not a problem.

But the one highlight of the afternoon was that I identified one of the Norwegians as my son in a past life, and I saw him undergoing a tribal initiation into adulthood. I broke down in tears, and sobbed, and when I was asked what I was feeling, I said "Pride in my son, for having reached this status". It was a very moving moment in the ceremony, which also affected my erstwhile 'son'.

Most of the lives I experienced during this initiation were as an aboriginal in Australia, but there was another fascinating incident, when I was taken back to a time in ancient Atlantis. I saw myself as some sort of regional leader, either a king or the equivalent, one of nine in the whole country, and I saw a little girl sitting on my knee. I knew that although I had a reputation as a

Reincarnation

very strict and firm personality, this little girl – my granddaughter – could "twist me round her little finger", and get what she wanted out of me. "Do you know who she was?" Asked the senior aboriginal lady. "Yes." I replied without hesitation, "She was you." "Correct." she said, "You were my *damu*." – using the Nyoongar word for "grandfather". So for the rest of my time there, she called me her "damu".

This had a very fascinating effect, for in aboriginal custom, anyone who is either an elder, or in some position where they are revered and honoured, is called by a family name, "Mother, Father, Uncle, Aunt", etc.; so the fact that the senior aboriginal lady – herself revered by aboriginals – was calling *me* her "damu", had the effect of lifting my status among other members of the tribe.

So my time in Australia that year had opened me up psychically in a way that I couldn't have experienced otherwise, and I now started to get my flashbacks into past lives more frequently. The first one came with Clare of course, and I identified her with two previous lives in ancient Egypt, both in healing temples, as well as in other more recent lives. Concentrating on Sybil, I felt that we had been in a deeply loving marriage in ancient Egypt, 3,500 years ago. Going back to Ann, the former lady whom I counselled and who caused me so much grief, I re-lived a fascinating life, and was given not only names and places, but also a year.

When I had first met Ann, I had had an inexplicable urge to help her financially, which I did, and when the link with her was eventually broken I grieved as much for not being able to *help* her any more as I did for the loss of her company. Weird. But when I was able to re-live our previous relationship, everything was explained.

The story began in 1544. At that time, at the height of the Renaissance in Italy, it was the custom for wealthy citizens to support the Arts by becoming patrons of artists, painters, sculptors or writers. At the time, in Genoa, there was a Signor Spinelli, a very wealthy merchant and ship-owner, who decided to do just that. He befriended and took into his household a struggling painter called Alexander. This young man was desperately poor, so much so that he was often forced to choose between buying food or artists' materials, but he had a wonderful gift for painting miniatures; so he was taken into Signor Spinelli's household, fed and lodged, and provided with all the materials which he needed, whenever he asked for them. But above all, he was given an entry into high society.

In those days, of course, there were no photographs so, when on a journey, the only way of remembering what someone looked like was to have their portrait painted, and since a miniature was a very handy way of carrying a likeness around, Alexander was soon in great demand, and prospered; so he vowed that one day he would repay Signor Spinelli for everything which had been spent on him.

But that was not to be in that life: Fate intervened, and one day, when Signor Spinelli was visiting one of his ships in the docks, a bale fell from an overhead crane and killed him instantly – and Alexander was inconsolable.

In this life Signor Spinelli incarnated as Ann, and Alexander as me, which explained why I couldn't do enough for her financially, and why I grieved because I no longer could. But several months after the incident, I was told, "Your debt is now re-paid". And my grief was lifted.

Less dramatic, but still interesting, we have a friend for whom I just cannot do enough. She has no need of financial support, but as she didn't drive, any time she wanted a lift anywhere I considered it my duty to take her. This continued for a year or two, and then I decided to try to find out why. I was taken back psychically to the 14th century, to what is probably now Poland, and shown two friends near a river which rushed through a steeply wooded ravine. One of the friends fell in, and his life was saved by the other. I was the one who nearly drowned, and our friend was my saviour, so it is no wonder that I can't do too much for her in this life.

I have a deep love for another friend, a lady now living at the other side of the world, and when I concentrated on her, I saw two little girls, possibly sisters, of about 11 and 12 years old. They were inseparable, and did everything together, but then I had another vision of one of the girls alone, a year or two later, deeply grieving for her friend/ sister. In that life we were those two little girls.

Reincarnation

Other flashbacks which I have had, at one time of my life or another, have been to ancient Egypt again, 3,500 years ago in the time of Queen Hapshepsut, to ancient Greece, ancient Rome, and twice to the French revolution; but the most interesting experience I had was a flashback during a regression.

"Regression" is going back, under the control of a hypnotist, to re-live a past life experience, and many years ago I had this experience. I should confess that I have a horror of wasting food. This may be explained in part by being brought up during the Second World War, when food wasn't in plentiful supply; I remember that, as a boy, I was always feeling hungry, but today, when food is plentiful, there is no such compulsion to save food, and yet I do. Why is that? The regression explained it all.

I was taken back to mediaeval times, when I was a peasant in some foreign land or other, and I was hungry, very hungry, and almost starving; so I broke into a food store – possibly a "tithe barn", where the year's harvest was stored – to steal food, but I was interrupted, and killed the person who found me. Now I was a hunted man, and was forced to live off the land, and often was so hungry that I had to eat grass to survive. So that life gave me a permanent horror of wasting food, and even today, after a meal, the only things left on my plate are those which are completely inedible.

I passed my strange ideas on to my children when they were young, as I told them that if they didn't eat all their "teenie-weenies (scraps off their plate) those teenie-weenies would run after them all day, shouting, "Hee, hee, you couldn't eat me". I spoke recently to one of my grandchildren, now aged 26, and she told me she used to be terrified by the thought that this could happen, so she scrupulously cleared her plate every meal.

So there are the facts; I am often asked if I believe in Reincarnation, but with me it isn't a mere belief. I know for a fact that it is true, and I have outlined here a few of my experiences. I have detailed my whole philosophy on Reincarnation in one of my books, "A Spiritual Primer", so I will not repeat it here, but at least I have explained the experiences which have led me to my conclusions.

Chapter Fifteen:
The Reincarnation Parable

I have spoken about my firm belief in the truth of Reincarnation, and have explained how I came to it through a long series of flashbacks in my life. However, there was one bit of direct spiritual input which clinched the matter, once and for all. In this book I have tried to avoid writing about spiritual philosophy if it was not directly connected to events in my own life, but in this chapter I will indulge myself and print what I was given – a modern parable – exactly as I was given it.

About 15 years ago I was asked to give a talk on Reincarnation at an Afternoon Guild in a Spiritualist church. I had given a talk there before, and I said to my wife, "The last time I gave a talk there, half of them were asleep before I had finished: but then, most of them are fairly old – some must be nearly seventy". (These days, someone who is not yet seventy seems to me to be quite young: how perceptions change as we grow older.)

I asked my inspirers for something to hold the interest of the congregation, so that they stayed awake for the hour, and they gave me this parable to explain Reincarnation.

Once upon a time there was a land in very mountainous area. The people there lived a miserable existence, having to work hard to scratch a living out of the difficult, stony soil. The country was totally ringed by mountains, and the people were cut off from contact with any others anywhere – so they thought that their own land was all that existed in the whole world. No one knew how their ancestors had originally reached this desolate country, but there were ancient legends which told of a journey from a far distant "land of milk and honey", which the ancestors had originally inhabited. Some great catastrophe had taken place there, which meant that the people had been forced to leave, and ever since that time their descendants had lived out their pitiable existence in this poor mountainous terrain.

Then one day there was great excitement in the country, when mysterious posters appeared all over the place inviting the people to take part in a journey back to the land of their original ancestors, which they were told was called "Paradise". They were warned that it would be a long, hard journey, but when they arrived they would find themselves in a state of happiness such as they had never dreamed of before, in a place where life would be perfect in every respect. All they needed to do was to enrol to go on this journey, and the rest would be explained to them in due course. Naturally everyone wanted to go, so they all enrolled.

When they had enrolled, they were all transported to a huge building, which they were told would be their "hostel" – their base for the journey. They were shown to their rooms, had a meal, and then went into a large briefing room, where they were told of the conditions which would apply throughout their journey — and these seemed to be very strange. The first was that the journey would take a very long time, and they would be travelling for many months. After the briefing, they would be shown a map of the overall area, and would be invited to choose the way which they thought would be the best one to take for the first day's journey. They would have advisors to help them, and to tell them the general direction of Paradise – the "Promised Land" – but the advisors would not have the power to tell them which way was best: they would have to make that decision for themselves. However, the advisors would be allowed to tell them what sort of equipment and clothing they would need, according to the different routes each one chose. Then the next day, before setting off, they would be issued with whatever clothing and equipment they would need, and food and drink for the day, and everything would be put in the rucksack with which they would also be supplied. Then, when they had studied the map one last time, they would be told to memorise their chosen route well, as once they started the map would be taken away from them.

The second condition was that every night they would be picked up from wherever they had reached and taken back to the hostel, where they would meet their advisors once more – but the next morning they would have to start from the same place which they had reached the previous night. When they met their advisers at night they would be shown the map and would see what they had wanted to do – and what had in fact happened. They would then be able to discuss what progress they had made, where they had gone wrong and strayed from their planned route, which parts of the day's journey had gone really well and – most important of all – what they intended to do the next day. They would have to choose their route again – remembering that they had to start from where they had left off – and would have to memorise the map once more, as it would be taken away before they started the journey.

Everyone was still willing to make the journey, despite the strange conditions, so on the next morning they all set off. Some walked fast and with purpose, intending to make the best progress possible during their first day, while others dawdled and dallied, reasoning that if they had a journey of several months before them, they didn't need to go very far on each day. Most kept to the main road which led away from their starting point, but one or two took some of the minor side roads, which they had previously calculated would be short cuts and would save time. All went well for the main party until they came to the first major fork in the road: some remembered which way they had planned to go, but many had forgotten, and so the parties on the road split up, going their own separate ways. This process continued at every fork in each road, until there were travellers scattered over a wide area.

At the end of that first day's journey the travellers were picked up, tired and weary, and taken to their hostel for the night, to be fed and watered and to have their planned meeting with their personal advisors. Some had kept to the main road all day, and had achieved what they had hoped, while others had pushed themselves hard and were in fact far beyond their original planned destination for the day. But whatever had happened, all were faced with the necessity of planning for the next day.

When they met their advisors, they were shown the map again, and the place which they had reached was indicated – and many realised with horror how far they had strayed from their planned route. The general road led upwards and round the mountains, but many had taken side roads which led them in a downwards direction, and so they now had to decide how to get back to where they would have been had they followed their original plan. They could, of course, just retrace their steps and go back to the start, but that would mean accepting that the first day's journey had been totally wasted – and none of them wanted to do that; so in most cases they chose a rougher path to get back to the original road – or even chose to abandon all paths and just scale up the hill through the tangled undergrowth in order to get back on course as quickly as possible.

They soon got into the daily routine of planning, travelling and then resting each night, while surveying the progress they had made. They always travelled in the company of others, but usually it was with people they didn't know. Sometimes, however, they met people with whom they had travelled before, and their reactions to them depended on what they remembered of the previous meeting. If they had had a pleasant journey together, or if the others had helped them in some way, they welcomed them with pleasure, but if the others had harmed them in any way, then their reactions were hostile from the beginning – although they could do nothing to stop those people from travelling on the same road as them. In fact, they usually found that when they met such people, *they* would be just as hostile in return. Occasionally they met a group of several people with whom they felt totally comfortable from the start – and only realised much later that they had all travelled together on a good day in the past.

More mystifying were the times when they met someone and took an instant dislike to the person from the start – and couldn't find out why – until at the end of the day they asked their advisor, who explained that they had had a bad experience with the person on one stage of the journey, but it was so long ago that they had completely forgotten it.

The travellers had realised from the very first day that there were little stalls from time to time along the road, and these stalls all proclaimed that they knew the best way to go to the destination. For a small fee such stalls would even give out what they claimed were accurate maps of the area. However, having bought such maps on one or two occasions in the past, and having found out that the maps were only partly correct, giving only a very limited view of a portion of the overall map, our travellers realised that the best way was to rely on their own memory and follow the route they had chosen personally before the start of each day.

Then one day, when they were fairly advanced on their journey, they found out a remarkable fact. Before the start of each day they had always been given all the tools and equipment they would be likely to need during that day's journey, and these had been put in the rucksack each carried on his back. One day, when examining the rucksack more closely than he had done previously, one man found that it had, built in, a tiny two-way radio, which was tuned into the frequency of the hostel where they all met their advisors every night – and he told the others in the party. From that time onwards, things became considerably easier, as when they were lost they could always tune in and get advice from their own personal adviser.

Another thing which they had realised by now was that they could take short cuts from time to time, without running the risks of losing themselves which they had experienced in the early stages. The road snaked backwards and forwards in a mountainous stretch, so they realised that by doing a vertical climb to the road above, they could save themselves many days' travelling, as the road would eventually lead round to that very spot. Granted, it would mean that they would have an incredibly difficult day's climb, but they would have all the equipment necessary to do it, and would be able to tune in to their adviser for help – so many decided to do exactly that, and voluntarily accepted one difficult day's journey in order to save many other days of time. In fact, the nearer that they got to their eventual goal, and the more they started to feel the "buzz of excitement" which that knowledge brought, the more they were likely to go for the short cuts and do far more than they would normally have planned for one day.

There was another strange thing which they realised after a long time on the journey: they started to occasionally meet people who appeared to have a great deal of knowledge about the whole journey, as if they themselves had already made it to the finish. Such people never told anyone what they *should* do, but were always available to listen to ideas and to stimulate the individuals to take responsibility for their *own* decisions.

The end of the story, of course, is that everyone eventually finished their own personal journeys – and found that all the legends were true, and that the land to which they came was the Paradise which they had expected: in fact it was far better than anything they could have ever wished for – and looking back over the many months of travelling they realised that it had all been worthwhile.

I was given that little story as a parable of our own journey back to the "Paradise" from which we originally came. We travel through a series of lives, each of which represents one day's journey, and at the end of each life we are taken back to the "hostel" where we are allowed to rest and take refreshments. We then review, with our own Higher Self (our personal spiritual advisor), what we have achieved during that last life, the triumphs we have had and the difficulties we have encountered. We see how much of our original plan we have fulfilled, and we decide what we need to do in order to get back on track or to make even more rapid progress during the next life, as the case may be.

When we first come into any life, we have a master plan which we have conceived during our rest period, but as we go through the life we are often distracted from what would be our best way, and so we make detours or run into blind alleys, from which we have to extricate ourselves. However, nothing is ever wasted, as we learn from the "mistakes" we have made, and in learning we complete some of the lessons for which we came into life in the first place. Finally, we realise that there are never any real "mistakes" in life – there are only "learning curves".

The people in our life with whom we feel an instant rapport are those with whom we have travelled in previous lives, and of whom we have pleasant memories, whereas those whom we meet and from whom we feel an instant aversion are those with whom we have had difficult relations in past lives. It is interesting that the reason why they have been brought into this present life to meet us again is to see if we can resolve those past problems, so that we can wipe the slate clean and get rid of things which are holding up our own spiritual progress. (This, of course, works both ways, as we have been brought into their life with the same intention).

The stalls which we see along the way are the different religions, philosophies and "...isms" which we encounter in life, all of which claim to provide the only true way to get to the Promised Land. However, each of these mind-sets provides only a limited view of the Truth, the reality of which is far greater than any one of them could ever indicate. We can only see that Truth in all its complexity when we reach the end of our life, and when we are once again shown the overall map by our Higher Self.

Finding that all travellers carry a personal two-way radio, which came only at a late stage in the journey, is the realisation that each of us has a direct connection with our own Higher Self, and if or when we decide to start to use that connection we find that things become a lot easier in our own journey through life.

When the travellers got towards the end of their journeys, they started to feel the buzz of excitement which that brought, and realised that they could cut the journey by several days if they voluntarily took on a particularly difficult climb. So it is with us: when we become spiritually developed enough, we are likely to take on greater burdens during our life in order to make faster spiritual progress. This may be seen in the fact that many people who have enormous mental, physical or emotional problems in this life are in fact some of the loveliest and most advanced souls whom one could ever wish to meet. However, in the story all the travellers had always arranged to take all the tools and equipment needed for the next day's journey with them – and so it is in our earthly life: we always possess all the gifts and talents which are necessary to help us to get through our lessons - although many of us refuse to accept the fact on a conscious level. There is an old saying that "No-one is ever given a load which is too heavy to bear" And if we only accepted the truth of that and used the gifts which we have, we would find the inner strength to face many of the challenges of life which at times might seem insurmountable.

Finally, the strange travellers who appeared to have done the journey before are those enlightened souls (or Ascended Masters) who have in fact finished their cycle of earthly journeys and who have voluntarily either stayed behind or have come back in order to help humanity to progress onto the next stage of its spiritual journey. We are at the moment at the end of a cycle of evolution when the human race is on the verge of taking a massive leap forward in consciousness, and there are many highly evolved souls who have volunteered to come into incarnation at the moment with the express purpose of helping us to make that next quantum leap.

One of the heartening facts about the doctrine of Reincarnation is that it means we don't need to do everything in one life. In many religions and mind-sets, you have one chance, and one chance only, and if you "blow it", then you are condemned to eternal damnation. Once you realise that you have many lifetimes in which to reach the state of perfection the pressure is off. However, the doctrine of "Karma" still applies, and sooner or later, we must sort out all the problems we have caused in all our lives – although we don't need to do it all in one lifetime.

However, a belief in Reincarnation has other, more immediate results. One of the precepts of many religions is that of doing to others what we would wish they should do to us. If this idea just remains a platitude, to be trotted out and quoted when it suits us, or when we are trying to impress someone with our own spirituality, then it does not do a lot of good. However, if we realise that it is a real fact of life, (in fact, that whatever we do to others *will* be done to us,) then we can start to behave towards others in a different way, and treat them as we ourselves want to be treated in our own future – and this starts to have dramatic results in a short time. The "Law of Spiritual Interest" kicks in, and we quickly begin to reap the benefits of what we are doing – once again, biblically, "We reap what we have sown", or – to put it into the modern idiom – "What goes around comes around".

Another result of the doctrine of Reincarnation is that fundamentalism in any religious mind-set is seen for what it really is – ridiculous. If one can be a Muslim in one life, a Christian in another, then a Jew, Hindu or Buddhist in the next, the absolutism of each religion is obviously totally inappropriate. However, each religion has much to contribute to our overall understanding of the essence of what "God" (or whatever name we care to use) actually is – so seen from that perspective each religion has an important part to play in the spiritual evolution of the human race. Each one sees Reality from one viewpoint, and by looking from several viewpoints successively we have a greater opportunity of seeing more of the whole picture.

I am reminded of the old story of how a wise ruler in India once called together six blind beggars and said that he would put them in front of an object and ask them to identify it. Whichever one then identified it correctly would be given riches untold. The first beggar touched the object and announced confidently that it was a spear. The second was equally confident that it was a rope. "Not so", said the third, "It is a large leaf". Each of the other three had his own interpretation, one saying that it was a wall, another saying it was a tree trunk and the last one a snake.

Each one was wrong – and yet in a way each of them was almost right, as the object he touched was similar to what he had said. It was an elephant. Each beggar had touched a different part of its body – a tusk, its tail, an ear, a side, a leg and its trunk – and so had made his identification. The whole story could only be found by putting together all the different views – and no one had done that.

I think that it is symptomatic of our human condition that we are all searching and want to find *the* answer to the meaning of life. The problem is that there is not just one answer – there are as many answers as there are questions, and each of us has a different way of interpreting any one answer which is ever given. In fact, as there are over seven billion of us on the planet, there are those many views as to what the answers really mean.

I once heard a story about four men who wished to climb a great pyramid. They had been advised that the best way to climb it was by starting from one corner and going up the ridge of the pyramid, rather than by starting in the centre of one of its sides and going up its face. The only problem was - which corner to start from? They walked round to every corner in turn, and saw a crowd of people at each one, all extolling the value of starting from there and following their particular route. Eventually they each decided on the corner they thought best – and by chance each one chose a different corner.

Once they had chosen their corner, each one was congratulated by the noisy crowd at that point, and was cheered as he started to climb. However, as he got higher and higher the noise of the crowd faded away, and he could now concentrate on what he was doing. He saw others climbing by the same route, but found that they were not very talkative – they were all too intent on where they were going. The higher he got the more difficult the climb seemed to become, but he persevered and finally reached his goal on the summit – to find that all his friends arrived there at about the same time; so the noise and fuss at the start had all been useless, as it didn't matter which way any one of them had taken, they all reached the same destination eventually.

Doesn't this little story contain a lesson for each one of us? The lesson is that eventually we all have to make our own mind up, and decide which way to take, and we can't choose the path for other people, any more than they can choose the path we should take. Whatever we do is right for us, but may well be totally wrong for someone else – and vice-versa. The only thing we can do is to follow our intuition and do whatever we feel is the right thing – and let others follow their own intuition, without judgement on whether what they are doing is right or wrong. In fact, there is a verse somewhere in the Bible which says, "Judge not, so that you are not judged". If only we could all follow that precept what a different world it would be.

The other thing which one learns from this little story is that all the people who were making the most noise were those who were at the foot of the pyramid. Once the four men had started the ascent there was no one to tell them whether they were doing right or not. Isn't this indicative of much of human life? The ones who do the most shouting are usually not the most advanced on their own journey – if they were, they would be far too concerned with their own spiritual progression to worry about what others were doing about theirs. This ties in with what someone once told me about true gurus: the way in which you can always distinguish them from less spiritual teachers is that they will never *tell* you what you *should* be doing –– they will always *ask* you what you think you *could* be doing.

Chapter Sixteen:
Infinity Clairvoyance

I was now well into the most productive phase of my life spiritually, and as normal the next event came without any warning – we were "thrown in at the deep end". A friend of ours, who had once been president of a Spiritualist church, started up an independent evening of clairvoyance in a neighbouring town, and then moved the venue to a community centre in Torquay, and finally to a local pub, the "Farmhouse Tavern", which had a large function room. We followed her many moves, and stayed with her for some years, but then she decided to retire, and emigrate to the Canary Islands, and asked us if we would take over the running of the evenings. Neither of us had had any experience of doing this, but we took it on – and this opened completely new vistas for me.

Sybil took on all the "back of house" stuff, of course, the organising, arranging for mediums, keeping the diary, handling the finances, etc., while I – always a "front of house" person – "chaired" for the medium each night. For those who are not familiar with Spiritualism, the chairman/ lady for the night is the one who introduces the mediums, runs the demonstration, making all the announcements as necessary, and eventually thanks and entertains the medium after the demonstration. Once again, this showed the differences in the characters of Sybil and myself; she is the one who prefers to work in the background, and is highly organised, while I am a more "charismatic" person, ready to stand up and talk at the drop of a hat, and never at a loss for words.

We made several changes to the way that things were run, and decided that we didn't want to be a profit-making organisation. So therefore, the night of the first meeting in the next year, we held a "charity raffle", where everyone present was invited to name their own favourite charity, and all the names went into a hat. We drew out about four or five, and split up the total profits for the previous year into donations to the lucky charities, and forwarded cheques to them, mentioning the names of the people who had nominated them. Over the next few years, we gave away several thousand pounds in this way, to the delight of the recipients.

I said previously that I had been introduced to a new world where I met many spiritual people, but now what had been a trickle of new faces soon became a flood. As I said, there are about thirty working mediums in Torbay, and not only did I meet all of them, over the years I got to know most of them fairly well, and some are now long-term friends. I had never been particularly interested in the different styles of mediumship, as I have always been more "philosophy-orientated", but now I had the opportunity of studying the way that different mediums worked, and I learnt an enormous amount about what had previously been quite a "closed book" to me.

We continued to run these evenings for many years, and over time the Farmhouse Tavern became one of the leading centres in the Bay. But change was in the air, and I became restless, and felt the urge to move on. I didn't know how, or why, but I could feel the change of energy. Eventually, I decided that we would give up running the evenings, although we would still be associated with them, and we handed over their organisation to two friends who, in the way of all "new brooms", changed the way we had been running it, made improvements, and lifted the status of the meetings at the Farmhouse even higher. They decided to give the centre a new and trendy name, and called it "Infinity Clairvoyance", which it still is.

However, although I had made the decision to hand over the reins, I was the one least affected, as I continued to chair each evening, as normal. But once I had made the formal decision, and I told my inspirers that we were giving up working, they said, "Oh, no you're not: we have more work for you to do – you have to write a book" and introduced me to a completely different chapter of my life, which I will explain in a moment. But before I do so, let me finish off the saga of "Infinity".

Having handed over the reins at the end of a year, we were immediately thrown into turmoil when we were told that the Farmhouse was being sold, and we would have to get out. Over the next few years we became wanderers, and had four different homes, three in pubs and one in a charity shop, before coming back home again to the Farmhouse, which had not actually been sold after all, as the deal had fallen through at the last minute. Through all these moves it was amazing how we never lost many of our regular customers, so we obviously must have been doing something of value for them, to make them keep following us around.

However, finally the Farmhouse *was* sold, and now we are housed in a new community centre, the Windmill, in Torquay, and are continuing to lead the field in the provision of Spiritualism. Each week we have a demonstration by one of a wide variety of mediums, then there are refreshments available, after which several kinds of healing are on offer, as is personal and/or bereavement counselling; for newcomers, or those who want to know more about Spiritualism there are "wise women" – usually mediums or former mediums – who can give information and help on request.

All of the above are free on demand, of course, but for anyone who wants a "One-to-one", a five minutes' reading with a medium for £3, we usually have the services of people with a wide range of disciplines; clairvoyants, Tarot or psychometry readers and a "Harmony Board" specialist – a lady who has introduced a completely new device through which information can be given. Among the audience was a professional reflexologist/ foot-reader, who was available for private consultations.

We are always on the lookout for people who are there for the first time, to make them welcome and help them to feel "at home" from the start. In fact, the whole atmosphere is more like a social club than a spiritual meeting, and though the demonstration is usually over by 8.30, on many evenings there are still groups of people sitting round and talking until almost 10.00. It is very interesting that although congregations in mainstream churches are dwindling, we have at least thirty people every Monday, and occasionally, when a particularly popular medium in performing, well over fifty.

All in all, I think that Sybil and I can be proud of the service which we have given to Spiritualism so far; we have been associated, either completely or partially, with the organisation of several hundred demonstrations, and we are not finished yet. I personally have now handed over chairing, and different people chair each week, in order to offer them an easy introduction to standing up in front of an audience, and Sybil is now a very accomplished and sought after, platform medium.

At the moment, I am suffering from severe Chronic Obstructive Pulmonary Disease, (COPD), due to having smoked heavily in my earlier life, so I am now flat-bound. However, this has given me the opportunity of reviewing my life to date, seeing what I have learnt, and what brought me to the conclusions which I now have. Therefore – as I have said already – even apparent disasters in our life may eventually prove to be of value in the long run. If, in fact, anything in this book has the effect of reaching, or helping, any of the readers, then I will be happy that that wise saying has been proved true once more.

I said earlier that when I announced to my inspirers, ("those upstairs") that I was retiring, they said to me that I had another job for me, I had to write a book – which now leads me on to talk about my venture into different Spiritualist work.

Chapter Seventeen:
Spiritual Writing

I wasn't a happy bunny at the thought of having to write a book at my "advanced" age (although this is now twelve years ago), but I was told that it would be a "channelled" book. I was told that there was a "committee" of sages and philosophers, from different periods of history, different cultures and different religions, who were waiting to channel through me, and all that I would need to do was to write it all down. I was also told that the contents of the book would be for the eventual benefit of humanity – and this interested me. I knew the story of the split between Science and Religion in the Middle Ages, which was resolved when one of the principle teachings of the Catholic Church, that the Earth was the centre of the universe, and that the sun and all the planets revolved round it, was finally disproved by Galileo

He had improved on the primitive telescopes in use at the time, and created a version which was far more powerful, and could show that the old ideas were totally wrong, and that the *sun* was the centre of the solar system; the Earth was merely a planet which revolved round it like the rest of the planets. After that, there was an uneasy truce agreed, in which everything of a material nature was the province of Science, but everything regarding philosophy was ruled by the church.

I had always believed that, one day, it would be proved that Science and Religion were just two sides of the same coin, and could mutually explain and support each other, so the possibility that in some small way I might be able to bring this about fascinated me, and I agreed to do the book. I thought that it might be a relatively easy task, but once more, I was proved wrong.

Spiritual Writing

I had become quite an accomplished speaking channel by then, and had no problems at all with standing up, letting my inspirers come through me, and speaking to an audience. Now, however, I was going to write a book, and that was completely different. Previously, in speaking, not only had I no control over what I was saying, but it didn't really matter – it was up to the audience to interpret what was being channelled. Now it was going to be recorded, written down and – in a way – it was going to become *my* property, so that I would become responsible not only for the words which were used, but for the meaning of the philosophy which was being given; so I had to understand what was being channelled, in order to possibly explain it to others later on – which meant that I had to learn it.

This was a completely "different kettle of fish", so the going was very slow. Not only did I find it difficult to do more than a few pages at a time, but also the inspiration didn't come regularly. Sometimes I would write several days in succession, while at other times there could be a lapse of between a week and a couple of months between sessions. All in all, it took about two years to write the book and a further year to have it professionally proof-read. However, eventually it was ready, and it was printed by an internet company, Lulu, in 2010. It is still available, exclusively through Lulu, via my website, www.wolfeagle.com. The ISBN code is 978-1-4461-0135-3.

It is possible that it will be revised and re-published at some time in the future. First of all, it was printed in ridiculously small 10-point type, and then, as it was published before the dreaded "2012", in the final chapter some of my own thoughts about the future have intruded into the channelling, so that chapter will have to be rewritten. If it is re-published, it would be through my present publishers, Stellium Flame, who are absolutely superb.

Although this was my first spiritual book, it wasn't the first book I had published. Many years ago the "Daily Mail" offered the chance to have a book printed as a promotion, and I was persuaded by Sybil to write my autobiography and have it printed. I did so, ordered a limited edition, and gave most of the copies to members of my family and close friends. Many years later, I was impressed to write another spiritual book. I was thinking about my own life, and some of the spiritual lessons which I had learnt, so I started to combine the two threads together, with the thought of eventually expanding it into a book. I didn't get too far at that time, but at least I had the germ of an idea in my mind.

Later, however, I was again impressed to write, and once more it was the result of a series of events, dating back two or three years previously. I explained earlier that Infinity Clairvoyance had a nomadic history a few years ago, moving to four different venues in about three years, and how we ended up in a charity shop. I also said that we had a core of an audience, about twenty in all, who followed us faithfully wherever we went; so after a couple of years or so, all were very well accustomed to clairvoyance. I was still chairing at that time, and one evening I was asked if I could think of giving a little bit of philosophy every week, after the demonstration, so I did, and over the next year I gave ten minutes of philosophy at the end of each session.

It went down very well indeed, and people enjoyed it. Each morning after the session, I made a typescript of what I had said the previous night, and gave it out the next week, so that people could build up their own little file of information, and this was greatly appreciated, and by the end of that year I had a collection of 48 typescripts, starting with basic information for absolute beginners and leading up to some quite advanced concepts. I didn't continue the talks – I think that soon after we had another change of venue, and the routine was changed – but of course I still had all the scripts on the computer.

Then one day I was looking through some old computer files and I came across the attempted re-hash of my autobiography, and I had a bright idea. Why didn't I combine this with the new material which I had produced in my talks, and make the two parts into a new book. I tried to meld them together, but it didn't work. I had often quoted the same events in both parts, but in different contexts, so that by trying to meld them, I would risk either repeating information, and over-stressing the facts, or by missing out important facts altogether. However, my inspirers then gave me the perfect solution: re-write the semi-biographical part as the main book, and condense the talks on philosophy, so that they could be added as an Appendix, in the form of a study course.

Spiritual Writing

So that is what I did, and the book was published in 2017, under the name of "A Practical Spiritual Primer". At a Spiritualist conference where I was speaking that year I sold quite a lot of the books, and from the feedback which I got they were very well received. However, the following year I got the best endorsement of all.

We have a friend Carolyn, who is one of the top three mediums in Canada, and she has an American husband, Ben, a very spiritual man, who is a book-lover and an avid reader of spiritual books. I sent a copy of "The Primer" to them as a present, and he came back to me later, saying that it was the best book on spiritual philosophy that he had ever read, so profound in content and yet so simple in explanation, and asked my permission to quote some extracts in a spiritual newsletter which he was currently editing. I gave permission of course, and was very gratified to have such a resounding endorsement from someone who is quite an expert on the subject.

The conference I mentioned above was also the cause of me writing my other book on Spiritualism, and once more it came about because of "a co-incidence". There was a very spiritual lady there with her partner, and both were involved in some sort of healing therapy, the name of which I can't recall. However, neither were Spiritualists, so I don't know what had impelled them to attend the conference. I had been booked to give four lectures, and she attended the first one, and came up to me afterwards and said how much she had been interested by the content, but as she didn't know anything at all about Spiritualism, she had a lot of questions about it. Could I answer some of them?

"By co-incidence" I had been thinking about the possibility of writing a book as an introduction to Spiritualism, and answering some basic questions about it, but I was a bit stumped when thinking what questions to answer; all the questions I could think of had answers which were (to me) so obvious that I couldn't imagine anyone asking them in the first place. However, I now had the solution to the problem; I could get real live questions from a non-Spiritualist, which could start me off; so I suggested that the lady wrote down her questions, and I could then answer them for her.

She came to my next lecture, the next day, with a list of questions. I had expected about ten or a dozen at the most, but she produced a list of about thirty, and I promised that in time I would answer all of them; so I came away from that conference with the basic layout of the book already done for me. It is now expanded to seventy questions in all, just basic facts, with little or no philosophy, but for someone who wants to know something about Spiritualism without getting into it too deeply, and it is probably the ideal introduction. It is only a small book of just over 100 pages, and is called "Spiritualism under the Microscope". I dedicated it to the lady who inspired it, and sent her the first copy. This was another example of the "co-incidences" in my life which aren't really "co-incidences".

Apart from this present book, I have another one in mind which I would very much like to do, but that is longer-term. I said that in my childhood I had an "out-of-body" experience, and I know that while out of the body it is possible to visit anywhere, either in our universe or in other dimensions, so if – or let's be positive *when* – I have learnt the technique of "Astral Projection" myself, I will want to go to the celestial "Halls of Learning", and study and learn more there. In the book, I would then describe what I had done, and what I had seen, and pass on some of the wisdom which I had learnt to the waiting world. It is a wonderful vision, but I have to learn how to do astral projection first.

Chapter Eighteen: Opening Out

When a woman desperately wants to have a child, we compare her to a hen who wants to sit on her eggs, and say that she is "broody"; but what is the appropriate word about a teacher, who desperately wants to teach, without the possibility of doing so? I have been a teacher all my life, from those early formative days at Sunday School, and now, bursting with all this new-found knowledge, added to what I already knew, I needed to pass it on to people; but how?

Many years earlier, Sybil and Clare had gone to a residential Spiritualist weekend at a holiday camp in Seaton, which they had greatly enjoyed. There were several hundred people in attendance, and over the two-and-a-half days, from Friday evening to Monday morning, there were demonstrations of clairvoyance, workshops on different aspects of mediumship, lectures on a wide variety of subjects, healing, private readings and much more. In all, there must have been almost sixty different events on offer, although individuals didn't have time to attend more than about a dozen.

Although I didn't attend that weekend, the two women came back so enthralled by their experiences that I decided to find out more about it. I learnt that it had been run by an organisation called L.A.D. Enterprises, (L.A.D. stands for Life After Death), which had been originally set up long before in 1986 by three of the great names of Spiritualism, Gordon Higginson, Doris Stokes and Jessie Nason, and by Derek Robinson, president of one of the foremost churches in England, the Wimbledon Spiritualist Church. The aim of L.A.D. was – and still is – to take Spiritualism out to the people, and although the original founder members have now all gone on to higher service,

Derek Robinson's family still run the Wimbledon church, another church at Hackbridge and also L.A.D. In fact, it is probably not too much of an exaggeration to say that these days WSC is the foremost "evangelical" Spiritualist organisation in the country.

This sounded like the ideal organisation to provide an outlet for what I felt I could contribute to Spiritualist evolution, so I contacted Ashley, a member of the Robinson family, who was the co-ordinator for L.A.D. and offered my services. To my great delight, he accepted, and in 2013 Sybil and I went to their next weekend, in a holiday camp in Weston-super-Mare. We both had an absolute ball. The energy was amazing for the whole of the weekend, and we thoroughly enjoyed meeting Spiritualists from all over the country, many of whom, of course, were from the Wimbledon church. I took some of my books, and was very gratified when several of them sold, and even more gratified when people came up to me later and said how much they had enjoyed my lectures. I then had the honour of being asked to speak at the big celebration, later that year, of the centenary of Wimbledon Spiritualist Church, and that cemented a relationship which I hope will last for a very long time.

That started my love of lecturing to large audiences on spiritual philosophy, and I have attended – and lectured at – several other conferences since. I feel that I will be working very closely with L.A.D. in the future, and have already an interesting scenario in mind, but first things first: I have to have my COPD healed, or if not healed completely, controlled to the level where it does not affect my ability to serve Spirit.

I continued to chair at Infinity, and then we had the other change of venue I mentioned, to the Windmill Centre in Torquay. This was a completely new area, which had never previously had clairvoyant demonstrations locally, so there were quite a few new people there who had never previously attended demonstrations. So, before the start of each demonstration I got into the habit of giving a little 5-minute introduction of philosophy, which was well received. However, as the COPD took hold, I found that after standing up and talking for just five minutes, I was gasping for breath and had to sit down again. So that little experiment came to an abrupt end.

Opening Out

The COPD progressed, to such an extent that when I did my four lectures, in the 2019 LAD Spirit-Seeker conference, I had to deliver them sitting down, which I found most inhibiting, as my normal mode of delivery is not only standing up, but actually walking up and down. Furthermore, on a couple of occasions at that conference I was forcibly reminded that I was no longer in charge of my own spiritual agenda. Before the start of each lecture, I told the audience that I could either stand and talk for five minutes, or sit and talk for an hour, so I would be doing the latter, and everyone accepted that. However, twice after a lecture, on the way back from the lecture theatre to the Foyer, where I stayed when not being needed elsewhere, I was stopped so many times by people who wanted to talk to me, that when I got back to the Foyer I collapsed and had to spend an quarter of an hour on my oxygen machine to recover.

Writing now, in the middle of 2019, the condition has got so bad that even walking from one room of the flat to another I become short of breath, and my visits to Infinity have become rarer, as even walking across from one side of the hall to the other is difficult, so I am being forced into a very sedentary life. While the down-side of this is that I now have virtually no social life, the up-side is that it has given me a lot of time which can profitably be spent on writing my books. As I have said, even apparent disasters in our life can have beneficial spiritual consequences.

Just in case I appear to be coming over as a "holier-than-thou" character, which I certainly am not, let me tell you of a little incident which helped to convince me of that spiritual truth. I spoke earlier about my use of invocations of spiritual beings, usually archangels, and said how powerful an effect they can have. So now I will tell you of the amazing incident which proved this to me, once and for all – and it happened in connection with one of the lectures I once did for L.A.D.

One year I had been asked to do four lectures; two of them were re-jigs of lectures I had done in previous years, which left me with a couple still to prepare. The third was no trouble, and I soon polished that off, but I had trouble with the fourth, on the subject of "Advanced Reincarnation". I couldn't get it right. I sweated over it for a fortnight, and it still wasn't right. I even typed the whole thing out – 36 pages of it – and couldn't find where it was wrong, but I knew that I couldn't give that particular lecture.

I went to the conference, not knowing how to resolve the problem, but hoping for inspiration; however, the answer still eluded me. Finally, in despair, twenty minutes before the start of the lecture, I sat outside the lecture room, script in my hand and asked for help. I was directed towards Gabriel, the archangel of spiritual inspiration, whom I had never used before, and I invoked him with my desperate plea for help. Suddenly, I felt a wave of complete peace come over me, and I walked in to do the lecture, threw my notes down onto the table, and gave what was probably the best one-and-a-half hour lecture of my life, completely impromptu. I was congratulated on it by several people on my way out, but then one very wise medium came up to me and asked if I knew why I had been unable to give the original lecture. I said, "No." and then she explained that there was one lady in the audience whom I would have completely destroyed psychologically had I given the lecture as planned.

That incident confirmed what I already knew, that we are always looked after spiritually throughout our life, and that if we would only trust, and believe that what I call "those upstairs" – which is in fact, our own Higher Self" – know far more about what is for our spiritual welfare than we will ever know, as they have the benefit of being able to see the past, present and future all at the same time., we will be helped. Therefore if – or preferably *when* – we accept the fact and "go with the flow", we are likely to have a far less stressful life than otherwise. It doesn't mean that we won't have "problems", but it does mean that we can face with them with a lot more self-assurance than we would normally have.

So that explains my philosophy, and my current state of mind. Although I have been assured by many medium friends that I still have a lot of spiritual work to do, I don't *know* that. It would be nice if their predictions come true, although it isn't important; but what I *do* know is that whatever happens to me will be for my eventual spiritual evolution. I have no fear of Death; in fact, in some ways I am even looking forward to it, as not only have I learnt a great deal of "the other side of life" over the last fifty or so years, but I have been given a vision of what my own spiritual future will be. I know *where* I will be going on "the other side of life", *what* I will be doing there, and I know certain details of my next life, like *where* I will incarnate, *who* my parents will be and *what* I will be doing in that life. Not only that, but I know that I will see my children again after I reincarnate. I will meet them and recognise them, although they won't recognise me. After all, our roles will be reversed: they will then be very old, whereas I will be a very young boy, (I will be male again next time.) However, the fact that I will be able to tell them long-forgotten details of their early life may well prove to them who I am. I am fairly sure that most of the children will accept it, although probably my Born-Again-Christian son won't, as to do so would prove that what he has fought against for most of his life is in fact true. But we shall see.

Chapter Nineteen:
More Counselling

There are some advantages in old age, but most people would say that there are more disadvantages. I am quite fortunate in that I am enjoying my old age, but the one disadvantage which I cannot escape is that the older you get, the more friends you lose. At least, you don't lose them, they just die.

One year, this was brought back to me sharply when there was a spate of deaths around us, some of whom were only acquaintances but others were close friends. Whenever a friend dies, I like to compose a little poetic tribute to them, which is often read out at their funeral, and it was while doing one, this particular year, that I started to think about the connection between Death and Spiritualism.

I realised that although the basis of Spiritualist belief and teaching is that there is no death, and the act of dying is merely a transition from one form of life to another, very little is ever said about death itself. Furthermore, although arguably death is the greatest recruiter into Spiritualism, as very few people ever think about even the possibility of an after-life until being shocked by the passing of someone dear to them, no-one in Spiritualism – at least, not to my knowledge – has ever thought about death as being an opportunity for recruitment; and certainly, there is no organised bereavement counselling service. So I started to ask myself how I personally would go about trying to help non-Spiritualists who were grieving, by giving them bereavement counselling.

When I say that there is no bereavement counselling service, I am talking about within the Spiritualist movement, as there are bereavement counselling services available in most local authorities. However, from the start I would want to distance myself from these, as all are obviously secular, and so say to clients (and I put this very bluntly); "Your loved one is no longer here, and that is the end of your relationship with him. Nothing can be done about that, but we will point out the stages of grief which you will go through, and advise how you can tackle them when they crop up".

From a Spiritualist point of view, of course, that is complete rubbish, as it is definitely *not* the end of the relationship, and while there will usually be a space of time before the loved one can make himself known, that will eventually come to an end; so in my method, I would want to be able to support the bereaved person, while giving the hope that there was something to look forward to at the end of the wait.

In all of this, I was acutely aware of what happened to me, when my beloved Eleanor made her transition. By that time, of course, I had been a Spiritualist for thirty years, so had no doubts whatsoever that she would come back as soon as she was able to, but I wanted to know what to do in the meantime, and I asked my inspirers.

I was given a lot of information, not only advice on what to do, but the reason behind doing it, so I will share this with you now.

When any two people are in a relationship, (any relationship, parent and child, marriage or partnerships, siblings or other family relationships, friendship, or whatever,) there is an unseen link between them. (I was given the term a "psychic bond".) The closer, or the older, the relationship, the tighter the psychic bond; that psychic bond is a bond of Love, in the true sense of the word; therefore, as Love is the material which forms the very building blocks of the universe, it cannot be broken, even by death. In fact, even during the lives of the two people it is often so strong that distance between the two people doesn't matter: whether the other person is the other side of the room or the other side of the world, it is still there, and can be felt sub-consciously.

My inspirers gave me a very interesting analogy of this. (An analogy is a simple every-day object or situation, something which can be used as an example to explain a more complicated idea.) They said that it is like having a pair of "walkie-talkie" radio transmitter/ receivers, tuned into each other's frequency.

You can contact the other person, but no-one else, nor can anyone else break into your conversations.

Now what happens when someone passes over is that temporarily they are unable to use their "walkie-talkie", as they are usually in convalescence. (I will explain that in a minute.) So what the one left on Earth does, thinking that there is no more possibility of ever contacting the beloved, is to switch off their own set, which leads to a hideous "total radio silence", that horrible feeling of complete emptiness which is initially felt by all bereaved people.

After an appropriate time, (more on that later,) the departed loved one is able to come back, and use their "walkie-talkie" again, but this time to no avail, as the one on Earth has switched their set off. Eventually, of course, by dint of trying over and over again, the loved one will make himself felt, although whether or not the one left behind will realise what is happening depends on their own spiritual awareness, and that easing of the "radio-silence" is the origin of the phrase, "Time is a great healer".

So that is what I was given as background information, so I said, "OK, so what can I do while I am waiting" – and was given the answer. I went to the photographer's with Eleanor's last photo before she passed, and he enlarged and framed it for me. I then put it on a dresser by the side of the bedroom door, and spoke to it every time I went past – and through it, of course, I felt that I was speaking to Eleanor. Sometimes I just said something simple like, "I love you". At others, I stayed there for minutes on end, pouring out my heart to her in ways I had never been able to while she was alive. (Men aren't usually very good at expressing feelings, and with my Aquarian detachment I had been worse than most.)

I was keeping the channel to her open for when she could transmit again, but even more importantly, I was *doing* something. I think that this is probably the worst part of the grieving process, the feeling that not only is there no Hope; there is nothing that anyone can *do* about the situation.

Before I carry on, let me explain two things that I said above. I said that the loved one would come back "at an appropriate time". So when is an appropriate time? The answer might surprise you: that depends on how ill the person was when he passed.

More Counselling

That sounds completely daft, doesn't it, as the person was so ill that he died, but here we must make a distinction. There are very many ways of dying, some very fast and others very slow. Just imagine, for instance, that you are walking down a street in a gale, and suddenly a tile is blown off a roof and falls on your head, killing you instantly. You are certainly dead, but equally you weren't ill moments before. In many cases you won't even realise that you are dead, and will try to carry on your normal life, getting increasingly frustrated by the fact that others aren't even noticing you, and are using your house, clothes, possessions, etc..

Now compare that with someone who has a long illness, something like a slow cancer or a dreadful disease like Motor Neurone Disease. They will be ill for a long time before passing – in many cases for several years – so that afterwards people will say, "It was a merciful release".

So why would these two different cases affect the length of time before the loved one could return? When we first go over to the other side of life, we normally go into a state where we are healed of our human conditions. There is no need of healing for the body, of course, as the body, and with it all its illnesses, has been left behind, but healing is still needed for our emotional and mental bodies, which have crossed over with us into the afterlife. The easiest way to understand what happens, with our human reasoning, is to think of those who make their transition as "going into convalescence" when first they go over.

In the latter case quoted above, the person has been devastated, mentally and emotionally, over a long period of time, knowing – and fearing – that the disease is terminal, and so the mental and emotional bodies will need a long period of convalescence. In the former case, where death was instant, there is no need of convalescence; all that is necessary is for the loved one to realise his new state.

Let me give you two personal examples. My beloved Eleanor had been fighting cancer for almost a year before she passed, and was totally worn out, mentally and emotionally, so she needed a long time – several weeks – before she could come back, but Sybil's mother was totally different. A sprightly 93-year-old, she had a fall, broke her femur, had a hip replacement, but passed three days later.

She had hardly suffered at all. She passed on a Tuesday, just after midday, but the next night, a mere 36 hours later, she appeared in the teaching circle of Carolyn, our Canadian medium friend, and said to the trainee medium who saw her, "Tell Carolyn to phone Sybil and tell her that I have arrived, and I'm OK." There are very many examples of loved ones attending their own funeral, as did Sybil's mother: she was seen by a medium doing a "Three Degrees" dance routine with two of her sisters in front of the coffin.

One of the most amusing stories I ever heard on this subject was about Joan, a very lovely spiritual friend who passed in her sleep. At the wake after the funeral, she was seen going from group to group of her friends, all of whom were talking and saying nice things about her. She was desperately trying to join in the conversations, but of course couldn't, as very few people could sense her and even fewer see her.

So, to go back to where we started, when I was thinking about the dire lack of bereavement counselling in Spiritualism, I was impressed to think of what I would do if I were doing counselling, and I drew up an outline of an approach.

I would certainly start with a brief resume of what I have said above, about the psychic bond, walkie-talkies and how to keep them open, but what would then follow? Here again, I was taken back to my own experiences, and the fact that I used Zadkiel when in moments of deep despair. I realised that the grief pattern of different individuals would be as varied as they themselves were varied, and that at some times they would be functioning almost normally, while at others they would be nearly suicidal, so I realised that I would have to introduce them to Zadkiel, and explain how to use him, while pointing out that he was to be invoked sensibly, not continually.

Looking forward to beyond the initial grief stage, and the realisation that the loved one was now trying to comfort the bereaved, was there any way that I could help them to actually *contact* the loved one? Here, of course, I ran into an immediate problem. If counselling Spiritualists, it would be easy to explain to them that before any spiritual exercise it was always necessary to put personal protection round you, but if one said that to a non-Spiritualist, it would possibly freak them out completely. So I had to accept that the first two stages which I have outlined would probably be as far as I could go with them. For those Spiritualists who hadn't sat in circle, I would have to give them a simple protection routine to carry out before going any further.

Finally, what about a ritual for joining with the energy of the departed loved one? That should go down well. Although many Spiritualists would love to know how to meld with their departed loved ones, there are probably very few who have ever done it, or would even know how.

So there were the four different elements of my bereavement package. I decided to write them up, and then had to find someone to test them on. We announced at Infinity that henceforth bereavement counselling would be available for anyone who wished to take advantage of it, and over several weeks I found that I had some clients. We reserved a small room, away from the hustle and bustle of the main room, and I practised my new skills. Most of the people I saw weren't very knowledgeable spiritually, but there were a couple who were, so while I went through the first two elements only with everyone else, I was able to go through all four with the latter, and found them very appreciative. I found out from experience that a basic session took about twenty minutes, and a full one half an hour, so that was information tucked under my belt for the future. At the end of each session I gave the person a typescript of what I had told him, so that he had something to take away with him, and I came away quite pleased with myself and my performance.

However, that was not enough; I had produced and tested a little bereavement package, so now I was anxious to go onto greater things, and I started to wonder if, or how, it could be brought to a wider audience. I just imagined taking it to a church committee, and asked myself what they would be asking me about it. Apart from the basic logic, of using bereavement counselling as a recruitment tool, I would need to tell them how to get started, how to set up an internal structure in the church, who should be counsellors, how to train them, and I would have to provide them with a basic script to guide them through the whole process; so I set to work to provide this advice package for churches, and in time wrote it all up.

A few years ago, just before Christmas, I was told of a lady who had just lost a beloved mother, and was grieving deeply, and

I was asked if I could send her a few words of comfort. I asked my inspirers, and they impressed me to write a two-page script of spiritual wisdom, which I sent to her. Apparently it helped her quite a lot, so I realised that this could prove to be a great help for anyone who was grieving for a loved one, not just at Christmas but at any time. Therefore I wrote up several versions, tailoring each one for a specific relative, father, husband, wife, daughter, etc., and after each session I gave the person a copy, specific to the dear-departed loved one, and I found that it helped, every time. So I went back to the package which I had made up for churches, and added a pro-forma which could be used as a template to be handed out to any bereaved person. A copy of this pro-forma, with instructions how to tailor it, will be found in the Appendix.

At the next L.A.D. conference, I gave a lecture on the subject, and several people, representing four or five churches, took typescripts of the whole package back to their own churches to pass on the information. I also did several individual counselling sessions while I was there, and found out that even experienced Spiritualists will sometimes have hang-ups which lead to them holding on to the grief, and not resolving it and moving on into a richer, more fulfilling, relationship with the departed loved one. One lady in particular, a working medium, found that the advice about setting up a photo, and talking to it, (and the reasons why,) led her out of grief which had been weighing her down for several years.

Finally, "by co-incidence", (which of course doesn't exist,) several of my Facebook friends suffered the bereavement of dearly-loved pets within a few weeks of each other, and I was drawn to think about "pet bereavement". I realised that for many people, particularly lonely people and old people, a pet provides a lifeline of companionship, and is often treated almost as a child, so that when that pet passes the person can grieve just as much as for a human relative. So therefore I wrote a little paper for those grieving for a pet, which included a ritual for contacting the pet's energy. I also gave information about the vexed question of "Does a pet have a soul?" – That often seems to bother many people, (including Spiritualists.)

So that was "a new string to my bow", and proved to me the truth of the old saying, "You are never too old to learn new things".

Chapter Twenty:
Suicide

Three of the private sessions which I did at the conference involved people grieving for loved ones who had taken their own life, and I was drawn particularly to those people, who I realised had a "double-whammy" of suffering on their shoulders. Not only did they have the normal grief which everyone feels, but they had the feeling of guilt associated with the idea, "Could I have done more to stop this happening"? So I developed a special little 'spiel' to help them.

To do this, I needed to go back to basic reincarnation, and show how we all have a list of experiences which we must have in order to learn all the lessons which are necessary to know everything about the human condition. In the Reincarnation parable, as those who were approaching the end of their journey sensed the nearness of "The Promised Land", they redoubled their efforts to get there quickly, often choosing particularly difficult day's journeys in order to shorten the overall journey. So let us look in more detail about the journey of all human beings.

We are all glorious spiritual beings, who come into human incarnation with the express aim of learning everything about what it means to be human. This is only a small part of our mission on the planet – the overall mission involves learning about – and experiencing - *every* life form on it, as I explain in detail in my notes on Advanced Metaphysics in the Appendix. Each experience will teach us a lesson, so when we come to the end of our life we will have learnt a number of lessons.

So how many experiences will we need in order to learn everything about being human? Well, there must be dozens of different ways of dying, for a start, ranging from dying in the most extreme agony to dying peacefully asleep in one's own bed – and we will have to experience every one of them. We will have to experience every pleasure, every pain, every disappointment, every success – in a word *everything*; so it obviously won't be accomplished all in the space of a single lifetime.

It is of value here to use a simple analogy, the analogy of a tick-sheet, where all the experiences we will have to face are listed. Now at the start, before our first incarnation, we have to choose which experiences we are going to have. We have no guidelines, as we have no knowledge of what being human means, there is no concept of "good" experiences or "bad" experiences. All are just experiences, so we choose a few at random, having exercised our Freewill and *predestined* ourselves to live in a framework which will give us those particular experiences.

For instance, if by chance we have chosen a life of abject poverty, we have cut off the probability of being born into a rich family, and a rich environment. If we have chosen a life with low intelligence, we have cut off the possibility of becoming a top scientist or philosopher, etc.; so we therefore have to choose our parents and environment to fit in with the basic experience we have chosen. Then again, most human experiences involve interaction with other human beings, so we have to find other people, about to come into reincarnation, whose own agendas will fit into ours in order to give us those experiences. This is why, when we come into incarnation, we have already *predestined* ourselves to the main framework of our life.

So we have our first incarnation, go back to the fourth (holding) dimension (I explain this in the Advanced Metaphysics section) to review what has happened, then tick off the experiences we have had on our "tick-sheet", and choose another lot, before returning into incarnation – and so it goes on, life after life. My own inspirers tell me that every human being will have about 2,000 lives, mostly – but not all – on this planet, before we have eventually finished our current mission on Earth.

However, although when we started we had no concept at all of the difference between "good" experiences and "bad" experiences, as we progress through a multitude of lives we learn

Suicide

that – in human terms at least – there *is* a difference. So thereafter, when making our choices before each incarnation, we tend to put off the really difficult experiences to a later date. (Just think about your own life: if you have a number of jobs to do, some easy, some difficult, which would you choose to do first? Some people would say "the difficult ones", but the majority would go for the easy ones.)

This means that in many cases the most difficult human experiences are left until the end of the succession of lives. Think about that. What are the most difficult life experiences of all? Arguably, the worst are those which involve physical or mental disabilities, or in extreme cases, both at the same time. Yet those who work with people having these are usually amazed at how spiritual they are, how absolutely loving and caring, despite their own problems.

So that sets the scene for us to think about people who take their own life, and to understand why they do it. As I said in the parable, when the travellers came towards the end of their journey, they started to "get the buzz" of how near they were to arrival, and to take more extreme steps to shorten the journey – and the same applies in human life. Coming into the last few incarnations, we know that we have to "tick-off" all the remaining experiences on our tick-sheet, so we do. However, sometimes we are a bit too optimistic, and we take on too much, and sub-consciously regret it in the actual life.

Where the person is in a spiritual atmosphere, and has a lot of spiritual, emotional and mental backup, he is likely to pull through the experiences without too much difficulty, and will in fact make enormous strides in his spiritual journey, but where he is not, then everything becomes too much for him, and he thinks that the only way of ending his torment is by ending his life. (On a subconscious level, going back and not taking on so many problems next time.)

When he eventually does that, those whom they leave behind are faced which this awful "double-whammy" of grief which I mentioned above, so what can we say to those who are grieving such a loss? Well, the first thing that we can do is to point out that the loved one was – or rather *is* – a very advanced soul, probably

157

more advanced than many others around him in his earthly environment were. Also, he has been totally honest with himself in accepting that he "bit off more than he could chew" before coming into life. Finally, far from taking the coward's way out, as most judgemental people would say, he has been very brave, and has ended this life with the intention of finishing all the remaining experiences fewer at a time than he had chosen in this incarnation.

So what can we all learn from that? Well, for a start, we can learn not to condemn others. They have their path to take, and we have ours. One famous Christian quote is, "There, but for the grace of God, go I", and a current saying is that you should never condemn anyone until you have walked for a mile in his shoes: an unusual idea, but very thought-provoking.

The second thing we can learn is that very often those who contemplate suicide do not really want to die – they want help, (which is of course what our health professionals tell us). But the professional help available is far too thin on the ground, certainly in this country, and there is a massive wave of need which is totally overwhelming it at the moment; here, it is appropriate to ask what it causing this need.

This is where we must go back into the spiritual: for the last few years there has been an immense wave of "spiritual consciousness" flowing across the universe and hitting the Earth, and it has affected all of us. Everyone has been affected by having their sensitivity increased, which has shown itself in many ways. On the good side, it has led to a dramatic interest in spiritual matters, and in the idea that this life is not all that there is. There is a huge increase in interest in clairvoyance, largely helped by the more relaxed attitude of TV program-makers towards showing fictional and factual programmes on mediumship and the supernatural.

This has led to many more people coming into Spiritualism, and to those already in it being more willing to sit in development groups to explore and/or develop any spiritual gifts which they may have. A further result of the heightened consciousness is the movement of many people into joining religious movements. However, on the down-side of the heightened sensitivity, many of those who are already involved in any religion or philosophy are being impressed to become more extreme, so we are seeing the rise of fanaticism in religion – all religions – everywhere. (Even many scientists are becoming more fanatically anti-religious – one has even vowed to destroy Christianity.)

However, most of the population are sitting on the side-lines, wanting something to hold on to in order to make sense of an increasingly senseless world, and I believe that the time is not very far off when a revelation will come which will radically change their thinking.

The discussion about suicide has led me on to speculate about broader issues, but I hope that what I have said might resonate with those of you who have been affected by such a bereavement, and help to relieve your grief somewhat.

Chapter Twenty-One:
Introduction To Metaphysics

This chapter is all about Metaphysics, and explains how I got into it. However, I realise that most people have never even heard the word before, and those who have heard it have only a very sketchy idea of what it is all about. Therefore, what I am going to do is to take you through the process that I myself went through when my inspirers were teaching me, and I warn you that this involves some scientific facts, which may prove to be difficult reading for some people. However, if you do manage to read it to the end, as I hope you will, I am sure that you will benefit from the experience, as I did.

Let me emphasise from the start that I am no scientist. The height of my scientific achievement came almost 75 years ago, when I was in my first term at grammar school. We all had to do General Science, a basic introduction to the various scientific disciplines, and we started with Biology in the first term – specifically Human Biology – Reproduction. I was fascinated by the subject, and studied hard, so much so that at the end of the term I came top in the class. It was an achievement never to be repeated, and today I can't even remember why on earth I found it so fascinating. But then, that is the trouble with old age – you lose your memory. (You also lose a lot of other things, but as far as I am concerned now memory is the most important.)

So when I came to channel my first spiritual book, I was faced with information which I didn't really understand, and I found it quite hard to do, as I said earlier. However, the book was eventually finished and published. At some time afterwards, I saw a TV series on Science, fronted by Professor Brian Cox, and found it very interesting, and when I later saw that he had written a book about quantum physics I bought it. I didn't understand most of it, but I suppose that I picked up enough information to at least know some of the basic vocabulary which he used.

So what is Metaphysics, and how did I get into it? Well, to answer the first question, arguably the greatest of all philosopher/ scientists ever was Aristotle, who lived in Ancient Greece in the 4th Century BC. He wrote over 200 learned papers on a wide range of subjects, scientific and philosophical, and almost two hundred years after his death the whole lot – or at least those which still survived through copies and commentaries – were catalogued by a man called Andronicus. He split them up into two sections, the "physical" books, which were scientific, and the non-physical ones, which were philosophical. Commenting later, Andronicus used the Greek word "meta", to describe these later books, and scholars for the last 2,000 years have been arguing over the precise meaning of what he said, as "meta" can mean two things, "after" and "beyond". So what he said can be taken to mean either "after the physical books", or "beyond the physical books". In our modern age, it is usually taken to mean the latter.

So "Metaphysics" means what is beyond physical Science; but it is also beyond Religion. In fact it is the area in which Science and Religion meet, and where – if they ever do – scientists and theologians (religious scholars) will find that they can start to understand one another. Over the last twenty years or more, there has been a split in both the scientific community and the religious community, in which the extremists have become more extreme, but some of the others have started to become more open to the views of the other side. There are virtually no scientists who have any religious understanding, and very few theologians who have scientific training, but on the fringes of each community there are some from both sides who are not too far apart.

I have always believed that one day the two apparently opposing views would come together, which is why I was so interested when my inspirers said that my channelled book would be for the eventual benefit of mankind, but although I knew of both sides, I could never put them together, until a couple of years ago, when I was writing "The Primer", when I suddenly had enlightenment. This is how it happened.

One day, taking a break from writing, I was just musing about the word "God", and I asked myself, "Who – or rather what – is God"? For some reason I was taken back to many years before, when I sat for a time in an Anglican Bible study group. Then I remembered that one particular passage always intrigued and puzzled me: the opening verses of the Gospel according to St John. "In the beginning was the Word, and the Word was with God, and the Word was God…..". What on earth did that passage mean – and what was that Word? Thinking about it once more, I asked my inspirers what that Word was – and I was given enlightenment: the word was "Energy". So now the amended passage reads, "In the beginning was Energy, and Energy was with God, and Energy was God. And by it were all things made, and without it was not anything made which was made."

Suddenly the passage makes complete sense. St John was stating a basic scientific fact.

Now "Energy" is a scientific word, so if it is the correct word in that context, then when scientists talk about "Energy" what they say should bear some resemblance to what theologians (religious scholars) say when they talk about God. So let's see if they do.

- Scientists say that Energy has always existed, and will always exist: theologians say that God is eternal.
- Scientists say that Energy is infinite: theologians say that God is infinite.
- Scientists say that Energy cannot be created or destroyed: theologians say that nothing can be added to, or taken away from, God.
- Scientists say that everything was produced out of Energy: theologians say that God created everything.
- Scientists say that although Energy cannot be created or destroyed, it can be changed into many different forms: theologians say that God can manifest himself in many different ways.

Even on those few examples, it is obvious that when scientists talk about energy and when theologians talk about God, there is at the very least a strong likelihood that both sides are talking about the same thing – although of course each would vehemently deny the fact.

Now if you ask a theologian to define "God", to answer you he/she will use words like "almighty", "infinite", "omnipotent", "omniscient", "omnipresent", "ineffable" – and some might even describe the knowledge as "arcane" or "esoteric". Well, very few ordinary people will know the meaning of all of these words, and they certainly won't be in anyone's everyday vocabulary, so the likelihood is that you will end up by being more confused by the answer than when you asked the question in the first place. However, if you ask a scientist to define Energy, you will get a very detailed and precise answer which will, most importantly, be expressed in clear, everyday language, and so understandable by everyone.

Therefore, rather than try to find a definition of "God" by the normal – religious – route, it could well be of value to approach the subject from a completely different angle and study what scientists say about Energy, cross-referring to Religion from time to time. Then, having reached a final and complete definition, compare it with what theologians say about "God" and see if it all makes sense. So I did just that.

Scientists tell us that the whole of the Universe is composed of atoms, which are tiny bits of matter, so small that they cannot even be seen with the naked eye, but that if we were small enough we would be able to actually walk in between atoms. Now to a layman – a non-scientist – that takes a lot of understanding. However, there is a story about an American university professor of Physics, who hit on an ingenious way of demonstrating what it meant. (The story is fictitious, and has many variations, but the general reasoning is very sound.) This is how it goes.

Every year, at the start of his first lecture to new degree students, he stood a large glass jar on the table in front of him, and filled it with golf-balls. He then asked the students whether it was full or not. The majority of them said that it was, although some were dubious, seeing how many spaces were left between the golf balls. So then he produced a bag of dried peas, poured them onto the golf balls, shook the jar, and the peas filled the spaces. Same question, and this time more students agreed that the jar was full.

Next he brought out a bag of very fine, very dry sand, and poured it onto the peas, shook the jar, and the sand settled in between the peas – and now all the students were convinced that the jar was full. However, he finally took a large jug of water, poured it onto the sand – and filled the jar.

The professor then explained that whether or not the jar was full depended on the students" own "level of understanding", or "level of perception". He said that there were four different levels, ranging from the top (superficial) to the bottom (most profound). At the first (golf ball) level, the jar *appeared* full from the start, but looked at from all the other levels it was far from full. In the same way it *appeared* full at the peas and sand levels, but it was only undeniably full at the most profound – water – level. So therefore, at all the other levels the idea of "fullness" was an illusion.

Everything which we can see, looking round a room, to us seems solid: floor; walls; ceiling; chairs; tables; etc. However, each of these is solid only at the superficial level of understanding, the level of sensory perception. We think that they are solid because they *look* solid and they *feel* solid, but at all the more profound levels of understanding the idea of their solidity is a mere illusion.

So here is our first cross-reference to Religion, for in Buddhism the first principle is that "All Reality is Illusion" – exactly the words that the supposed professor used.

So we return to scientists talking about atoms, and ask, "What is an atom?" Well, first of all, where did the word "atom" come from? To find this we have to go back 2,500 years ago, to an Ancient Greek philosopher/scientist called Democritus. He theorised that if you took a piece of gold, cut it in half, then cut one of the halves in half, and repeated the process many times, you would eventually get to the stage where what was left was "ά τόμος" (a tomos,) which meant "not cuttable". Then in 1803 an English physicist named John Dalton joined the two Greek words, chopped off the tail, and formulated the word "atom", which he used in his new "atomic theory".

Well, that is where the word came from, but what are atoms? If we study an atom – any atom – under a very high-power instrument called an "electron" microscope, we see that it forms a circle, in the middle of which there is a central core, or nucleus. Spinning round the nucleus are a number of minute bits of matter called electrons. When I say "minute" I really mean it: each one is only about one-hundredth of the size of the nucleus, which is a tiny spot at the centre of the atom – which is too small to be seen by the naked eye.

The most interesting thing about, electrons is that they are all moving – very fast – round the nucleus, and wherever there is movement there is vibration. Therefore every atom in the universe is vibrating, so the universe itself is vibrating, and so is everything in it, including ourselves.

There is a very wide range of vibrations in Nature, from very slow to extremely fast, and human beings are capable of perceiving only a relatively small number. We perceive some of the slowest as heat, others as sounds and others, higher up, as light. However, with one exception, we are not able to perceive vibrations in any of the other areas in the range, for instance ultra-sound, infra-red, ultra-violet, X-ray, radio waves and so on; but all human beings have the ability to tune into a very small area of vibrations right at the top of the range, which is called the area of Extra-sensory Perception (ESP).

This is the area of very fast vibrations which is used for receiving information without the use of the normal five senses of touch, taste, smell, hearing and sight. Some people are particularly sensitive to these vibrations, and we give the name of "mediums" to such people. Now spiritualists are very aware of vibrations, and use the word frequently: Mr/ Mrs X, a clairvoyant, works on a very high vibration; Mr Y does psychometry, and picks up the vibrations from the objects which people give him to hold; Miss Z reads auras, and senses and interprets the vibrations of the different colours in the auras of her subjects. We walk into a room and feel its vibrations, or sit down next to a person and sense their vibrations. Contact healers pick up the vibrations of their patients, etc.; so here is a second connection between Religion and Science: Spiritualists teach about vibrations, and do exercises to raise their own sensitivity to them, while scientists explain what vibrations actually are.

At the beginning of the last century, scientists started to wonder if it would be possible to split an electron out of its parent atom, and started to design experiments with the aim of doing just that. The race to be the first to achieve it was won by an Anglo-New Zealander called Edward Rutherford, who succeeded in 1917, and earned for himself the title of "Father of Nuclear Physics". Fifteen years later two of his students were able to achieve another feat when they split a tiny part from the nucleus of an atom. The Latin word for 'small part" is "particulum", and so "particle physics" was born, and much of the remainder of the century was spent in learning more and more about the behaviour of particles.

It was found that when an electron was split from its parent atom, that action created a burst of energy, but when a particle was separated from its nucleus, the particle itself was a "packet" of energy. The Latin word for "packet" is "quantum", and it gave its name to completely new branches of Physics and Mathematics.

However, the more time that scientists spent studying Quantum Physics, the more confusing the picture became, for particles did not obey the basic laws of Physics which had been laid down by Isaac Newton more than 300 years ago. For instance, a single particle could appear at two different places at the same time, while every particle on earth could be proven, mathematically, to be in communication not only with every other particle on earth but also with every other particle in the whole universe.

Scientists have always had the dream of finding something to connect all knowledge into one super-theory – the Theory of Everything – but the more that they find out, the further away that dream becomes. They have currently identified more than 100 particles, and each one seems to have different properties.

So to sum up the last two centuries of scientific discovery in a few words, (and to relate them to the "levels of understanding" mentioned earlier,) the most superficial level – the "golf ball" level – was the formulation of atomic theory by Dalton in 1803. Next, the "peas" level was the splitting of the atom by Rutherford in 1917. The 'sand" level was the splitting of particles from a nucleus in 1932. But what is the most profound level, the "water" level"?

Into Metaphysics

This is where Science comes to a halt, for it is where we are at the moment. New particles are continually being discovered (a few years ago the scientific world was rocked by the discovery of the "Higgs boson", predicted by Sir Peter Higgs some 50 years ago), but the ultimate dream, the Theory of Everything, is still as far away as ever.

However, although it is at the moment the end of the known Science, it is only the start of the information in my book. For "the committee" tell me that there *is* a Theory of Everything, and it also is concerned with particles, but the particles are so different from the scientists" particles that the committee have given them a new name – ***primal particles.***

These primal particles have four main properties:

1) All of them are absolutely identical in every way;
2) There is an infinite number of them;
3) Every particle is in continuous communication with every other particle in the Universe;
4) Particles group together to make different patterns, each of which creates a "scientist's" particle. So therefore the primal particles are the actual "building blocks" of the whole Universe.

Now scientists might possibly accept this idea as an "ansatz" – an idea worth considering; in fact, the third property is exactly what they have already established for ordinary particles. However, they would probably have difficulty in accepting the fourth property, which would mean that there is a whole new range of particles (a "level of understanding") which is at present completely unknown.

But here we come to a totally new concept – new to both Science and Religion – and one which, when understood, will eventually provide the bridge between the two. Because each primal particle is not only a *particle of energy*, but is also a *particle of intelligence*. ***Intelligent energy.*** (Scientists might possibly accept the phrase "conscious energy", as they accept the existence of "consciousness", although they argue over its possible location.)

Furthermore, each particle of intelligent energy is also a particle of *life itself*.

So we now have an infinite number of particles of energy (infinite energy), which are also particles of intelligence (infinite intelligence) and particles of life (infinite life.) So if we consider the sum total of all the primal particles in the universe, we have something which is infinite energy, infinite intelligence and infinite life. Can you see where we are heading?

Let us now move away from Science and on to the English language: in our language we have "collective nouns", which are special words given to groups of things. So we talk about a "school" of whales, a "shoal" of fish and a "flock" of birds. We have names for groups of people also: a large number of people in the open air is a "crowd", a group inside, in a theatre, concert hall or lecture, is an "audience", while a group in a church or place of worship is a "congregation".

So what are we going to call the group which is composed of all the infinite number of primal particles of intelligent energy, life itself? Well, each major religion has its own word (or sometimes several words). But apart from those, many words and phrases have been allotted to this group over the centuries, such as The Almighty, the Eternal, the Supreme Mind, the Force, the Power, the Energy, the All-That-Is, the I AM principle, Mind and Spirit. However, the most common name in the Western world is the word **"God"**.

So now we can give a simple answer to the question, "What is God": God is the total of all the primal particles of intelligent energy, particles of life itself, in the universe. Furthermore, we can cross-refer with some of the words which theologians use to define God:

- *Infinite:* without any ending or limit: if the force is composed of an infinite number of particles, then it must itself be infinite.
- *Almighty:* this word means "able to do anything": well, any force which has infinite energy can do anything, can't it?

- *Omnipotent*: from the two Latin words, "omni" – meaning "all" – and "potens", meaning "able". Combined, they mean "all-powerful" – just a "posh" word for "almighty".
- *Omniscient*: once more from Latin; 'sciens" means "knowing", (we get the word 'science" itself from it,) so "omniscient" means "all-knowing". Well, anything which has infinite intelligence would know everything, wouldn't it?
- *Omnipresent*: all-present. The infinite number of particles is infinite in number and extent, so they are everywhere.
- Ineffable: the most difficult of all to understand – and one which most ordinary people have never even heard, much less understand. The dictionary definition is "too great or sacred to be given a name". Unfortunately, giving a name to the supreme force of creation limits that force, and therefore it is no longer infinite. It limits the force by saying that it cannot be xxx – the name that another religion gives to it. Throughout history wars have been fought over the correct name for the force and are still being fought today – and in some parts of the world even saying the "wrong" name is a short cut to a death sentence.

In some circles, knowledge itself can be described as "arcane": this simply means "mysterious". Well, had I started this chapter by saying, "What is God? It is all of the primal particles of intelligent energy, particles of life itself, in the universe" – you would have found that very mysterious, wouldn't you? However, now that you have had it explained, it is no longer so – the knowledge is no longer "arcane".

Finally, knowledge is sometimes described as "esoteric". This word means "reserved for, or understood by, only a select group of people". Throughout history religious societies have existed which have kept their knowledge a complete secret from all but their own initiates. One such society was the Essenes, an ascetic Jewish sect which existed at the time of the Master Jesus. In fact, there is a tradition among some Christian sects that he was taught and trained by the Essenes for much of his adolescence. Also, the Master himself chose twelve disciples, but within that number there were only three (or possibly four) to whom he gave the full range of knowledge.

So that is how I was introduced to Metaphysics, but it was only the start of what could be a very long journey. For those of my readers who are particularly interested, I have put a second step in that journey in the Appendix, but I warn you now, do not read it unless you are prepared to have your brain stretched in a way it hasn't been stretched before. It is definitely not for the fainthearted. However, for me it fits in completely with my Aquarian mentality, so that is what I am currently studying.

Chapter Twenty-Two:
Predestination And Freewill

I have mentioned my firm belief in both Predestination and Freewill, and have indicated a way in which they can be reconciled; before we come into life, we decide what lessons we are going to learn in that life – exercising our Freewill – but that then *predestines* us to undergo those lessons. Within the life we make many other decisions, once more exercising Freewill, and are bound by the consequences of those, but that can only happen within the overall framework of the predestination which was set in the pre-life decisions. The best way to understand this is to think about a set of "Russian dolls", each smaller than the last. The first and biggest doll is the original predestination, which governs the 'size" all of the subsequent dolls – in real life, the ability we have of affecting the overall pattern.

Throughout this book I have also stressed my belief that everything happens for our eventual spiritual benefit, and that it happens at the right time as well. During my time in Australia in 2004, I was told the aboriginal version of this – that everything happens when it *wants* to happen. For instance, someone will call a meeting to discuss something or other, but won't give a date or time. Then, when he is impressed by his inspirers, the meeting takes place. I was told – although I have no proof of this – that sometimes the time for the meeting might be fairly late at night. No matter, if that is when the meeting *wanted* to be held, that was it.

I actually had a strange example of this while I was there. It was Olive's birthday, and she was going to have a birthday party, to which I was invited. I asked at what time I should turn up, and was told, "Whenever you feel like it." – which I found very strange. However, as I knew we would be having a meal, I worked out logically that it would probably be some time in the middle of the day, so I arrived at one o'clock – to find that I was the first guest there. Over the course of the next couple of hours or so, others came, until finally, at about four o'clock, when the last guest had arrived, the party started.

I have mentioned several occasions in my own life when the timing which had been planned for something wasn't correct, but the most amazing example happened in the choice of the flat in which we now live. Many years before, Sybil had had a vision of visiting a friend, who was living in a very high block of flats, overlooking a harbour far below, and she saw that there were two flats available, so she said, "Keep one for me." Four years ago, we were living in a bungalow which had a large expanse of lawn at the front and a smaller paved and terraced garden at the back. I wasn't a "dedicated gardener", so the garden was getting a bit untidy – and quite honestly, a bit too much for me. The other thing was that Sybil's mother, who had lived with us for some time and had had her own room, had now passed away and although it was only a small bungalow, it felt a bit empty without her, so we decided to move.

We put the house on the market and, to our amazement, it sold immediately. The first couple who saw it came back two days later, saw it again, and put in an offer, which we accepted – but we were now in a quandary, as we hadn't even started to look for another house. Things became more complicated when Sybil had to go into hospital for a short time, and everything came to a halt, but eventually our buyers started to press for an early date of completion, so we had to do something positive.

I was always firmly set against buying a flat, and while Sybil was in hospital I went along to see a bungalow in a nice area, and fell in love with it. I told Sybil, and showed her the particulars, and she said, "Well, if that's what you really want, go ahead and put in an offer". I did, and it was accepted. When Sybil came out of hospital the next week, I took her to see it and, although she had reservations, she agreed to go ahead.

It was an amazing bungalow, absolutely immaculate. It had been on the market for £30,000 more six months before, but hadn't sold, so now the price had been dropped to within our price range, and that seemed a good indicator that it was for us. It had everything that I had ever wanted in a house. The owner, long retired, had been a skilled electrician/ handyman, had built a room in the attic and had added all sorts of electrical additions to the house. He was also leaving a fully equipped workshop in the large garage. The house had a very large lounge, which could comfortably accommodate about fifteen people – ideal if we decided to run home circles – and had two gardens, both fairly small and manageable. For me, however, the crowning glory was a small paddock at the back, which contained several mature fruit trees, and space for many more. I had had a small but very productive orchard at Iddlecott, so I could imagine having the same again in this new house. The only snag was that the complete site was on steeply sloping ground, with the top of the paddock considerably higher than the roof of the bungalow, but I was still fit and active, and didn't see that as a problem.

So we went ahead, and agreed a completion date with our buyers, but where were we to live while waiting to move into the new house? One of our friends stepped forward and offered to put us up for "two or three weeks", while we were waiting, so we move into one of her rooms, took as much hand luggage as we would need and put it in her spare room, and stored all the furniture and the like in the garage of our own bungalow, which the buyers said we could use until we moved into the new house.

As I said, Sybil had her reservations about the bungalow, mainly concerning the steepness of the slope, and my ability to cope with walking up to the top level, and these reservations were strongly supported by one of our medium friends, who was adamant that it was not for us. I was equally adamant that it was, and stubbornly refused to listen to anyone else. (Aquarius is a "Fixed Air" sign, and once they get an idea into their head it is very difficult to get them to change.) When I look back now, I can see that I was living in the past; twenty years before, it would have been ideal. It had everything that I had ever wanted in a house, and I might have been able to benefit from it. Now, it was too late; I couldn't see into my future, and my present problems of mobility, but "those upstairs" could, and so could the inspirers of my friends.

Then started the most frustrating period of our lives. When we told our estate agent who the legal representatives of our vendors were, he threw up his hands in dismay and said, "Oh no, not them: they are the worst people to deal with in the business" – and that is how it proved to be. There was delay after delay, and months passed for our solicitors to get replies to some of their legal queries. Then, eleven weeks later, our host friend said that she was going to have to ask us to move out, as she had major structural work scheduled for the following week, and would need our rooms. Fortunately, another friend, who lived in a large block of flats overlooking the harbour, stepped in and said that we could stay with her for as long as we wanted to, as she lived alone and would like a bit of company; so we moved in with her.

However, I had had enough of the delays to our purchase, so I told my solicitor to give the other party an ultimatum, that if we didn't have completion by a certain date and time, we would pull out. They didn't, so we walked away. Now, of course, we were back to the situation we had been in four months before, and had to look for new accommodation. But we both liked the atmosphere of our friend's flat so much that when she said that there was a flat up for sale in the same complex, we contacted the agent and went to see it. It was quite nice, but didn't have any "wow" factor, so we declined it. The agent said that there was actually another flat in the complex, but unfortunately only for rental, so despite my reluctance, we went to see it.

As soon as we walked in, Sybil said, "This is mine." It was a two-bedroom flat, overlooking the harbour and part of the bay beyond, and it was absolutely immaculate, freshly decorated throughout and with new carpets and curtains. We told the agent that we would take it, but he said, "Well, there is a snag: you will have to be vetted by the owners." This sounded a bit strange, but we arranged to meet them the next day at the flat. The first question which they asked was, "Do either of you smoke?" We assured them that we didn't, and after that we got on like a house on fire. We liked them, they liked us and agreed to let it to us, and we signed the tenancy agreement two days later, and moved in the same week. We have now been here for almost four years, and have never regretted a moment of it.

174

Predestination and Free Will

So why was all this an example of predestination, and not just another co-incidence; because four months before, when we moved out of our house, the flat was still occupied by the previous tenants, who were both heavy smokers. They gave their notice in and moved out, but the whole place stank of tobacco, and had to be completely gutted, de-fumigated and redecorated, with carpets, curtains and everything replaced. So that when we moved in it was as though it were a new flat. Do you still wonder that I am convinced about the truth of predestination?

Appendix

Author's note: This chapter has been inserted for the benefit of those readers who have understood and enjoyed the chapter entitled "Introduction to Metaphysics", and have a real interest in knowing more about the subject. It introduces some very advanced concepts, and as such is not suitable for the average reader, as it requires a lot more concentrated thought – it is certainly not just "light reading". If you are not prepared to have your mind really stretched, then I suggest that you skip the whole chapter and go on to the final chapter, "The story of Numan"; this is considerably easier to read, and probably far more interesting, as it deals with the spiritual journey of each human being, from first incarnation to the final progression off the planet, as a perfected soul..

Chapter Twenty Three:
Advanced Metaphysics

In the chapter introducing Metaphysics, I spoke about primal particles. These are the particles which are the building blocks of the whole Universe, and have very special properties. First, there are an infinite number of them, and every one is identical to every other one. Also, every one is in continuous contact with every other one, and with 'Source", the ultimate level of purity, Love, call it what you will, in our universe and in every other universe. Every particle is also a particle of energy, of intelligence, and of life. The natural "home" of all particles, when they are not working, is in the tenth dimension, although when on assignments they may move into every lower dimension at will.

One day, a huge number of particles sensed a thought from Source. "It would be interesting to go to a tiny planet, in a small solar system, in an outer arm of a galaxy at the edge of the third-dimension universe and study every life form, find out if there was any chance of it evolving into something else, and if there is, help it to happen". A thought from Source was the equivalent of a command, and so this vast cloud of particles started to travel down through the dimensions, through the fifth, the lowest spiritual dimension, and through its portal with the fourth, which barred all negative energy from going up into the spiritual dimensions, through the fourth, a "holding" dimension, where human life-forms stayed in between incarnations, and then into the third dimension, the only one where it was possible for life-forms to have physical bodies.

None of the particles had ever experienced physicality before, so they all chose to start in the most alien life form of all, one which did nothing, had no movement, no growth and could not reproduce itself – a mineral. They combined together in different patterns, and became a physical particle of an atom of one or other of the minerals, and experienced that until eventually the atom decayed and released them. They then re-formed into another kind of particle, in an atom of a different mineral, and repeated the process.

After eons of time, they had all experienced existence in every mineral life form and knew everything about every one – they had actually *been* that mineral – and they realised that there was no possibility of any of the minerals evolving, so they moved on to a different class of life forms – what we would call the Vegetable Kingdom. These were far more interesting. First, although there was only very limited movement in most of them, there was growth, and there was reproduction as well. Next, whereas every atom in a mineral had been identical, there were many different elements of most of these new life forms, roots, stems, flowers, seeds, etc., so there was far more variety. Finally, the best thing about them was that they had a very limited life-span, compared with minerals, and so change could be introduced into succeeding generations of them relatively quickly.

Once more the particles joined with others, and formed patterns which created physical particles, part of an atom of an element of a plant. Let us imagine that they became part of a root. After a time, having experienced being *part* of the root, they moved out of physicality and became part of a "unit of consciousness" of that root. A human analogy would be someone who has been doing a job for a long time, and has been promoted to foreman because of his experience. As part of a root's unit of consciousness, they were able to consider how the root worked, how it coped with stresses and different environments, and to work out ways that it could operate more efficiently, and store that knowledge for the future. Then they moved on to become part of a different element of the same type of plant, possibly the stem.

Once more they experienced a time in that element, then moved on to being part of the "unit of consciousness" of that element, and stored even more knowledge, before moving on again. Eventually, having experienced existence in every element of the plant, they became part of the "pool of consciousness" of the plant – in human terms, becoming senior foremen – and were able to consider everything about it. What were its strengths, and what weaknesses did it have. How could its strengths be improved, and its weakness reduced, if not completely eliminated. Would lengthening the roots to give it greater hold on poor soil be of value, or doing something to improve the viability of the seeds, or ways they were dispersed help – and such questions. Finally, having discussed all the possibilities, working on a particle level they were able to "tweak" the DNA in the seeds, so that the next generation of plants would be better able to withstand the problems the plant faced. In that way they helped the plant's evolution.

Each particle then moved on to another plant life-form, and repeated the whole process, until eventually, after many millions of years, they had experienced life in every type of plant on the planet, and so they moved on to what we call "the Animal Kingdom". This was even more exciting than the Vegetable Kingdom, as there was far more complexity in animals than there was in plants, and also every animal had more developed forms of consciousness than had existed in plants, and greater abilities of movement. However, the basic process was still the same as it had been previously, first choose a subject, in this case an animal, then choose an element of the subject, a bone, muscle, nerve, etc., experience life for a time as that, and then become part of its unit of consciousness.

Now, however, with the greater complexity of animal forms, there were many different levels to go through before reaching the ultimate level, the pool of consciousness of the complete animal, so the whole process took much longer. However, the end result was still the same, the animal's strengths and weaknesses had been studied, and tweaks of its DNA meant that it was helped to evolve in future generations.

The next step, when everything had been studied and learnt about every animal, was to move on to human beings, and initially everything was very simple. After all, there is not much difference between an animal and a human being in the basic physical make-up. Both had bones, muscles, nerves, skin, teeth, nails, etc., so this stage was passed without too much difficulty, and the basic evolution of the physical body was carried out over a few hundred generations. So now the particles came to the final task, learning everything about what it meant to be a *conscious* human being, in charge of his own life – and this would prove to be far more difficult.

This is now the subject of another chapter, and another story – the story of Numan.

Chapter Twenty-Four:
The Story Of Numan

Numan was very excited: He had originally come to Earth, eons ago, to learn everything about all the life forms on the planet. He had experienced existence in every mineral, plant and animal form, and in the various parts of a human being. Now – for what was scheduled to be the last life form – a large group of spiritual particles had come together to create the consciousness of being a complete human being. All of these particles were identical, and thought alike, so for practical purposes we can think of them as one entity – Numan.

(Numan is an abbreviation of "New human". Numan could have been either male or female – the overall journeys would have been identical – but for ease of writing, I am going to assume that he was male.)

It was no wonder that he was so excited: after a vast time on Earth, learning everything about every life form, according to his original briefing before he started on his mission, he was about to become a human being, in full control of all the parts of his body, and having all the experiences that a human being can have. According to the information which he had been given, what he thought of as his "instruction manual", he would only need to be in this last life form for about eighty years, after which he would be free of the Earth and able to travel back to his original home.

So he consulted the blueprint which he had been given for creating a human being, and saw that he would have to craft three separate subtle bodies, spiritual, mental and emotional. These would eventually be attached to the physical body to create the complete human being, and he had an unlimited supply of primal particles which he could use as the raw material with which to work. Well, the first body was easy enough: it was just a question of organising the basic material into a coherent shape, and that was it. But the second was far more complicated: the vibratory level of the primal particles was far higher than that of the mental body he had to make, and the gap could not be bridged directly by stepping down the rate; so an intermediate body had to be created, what we would in modern language call an "interface", before the mental body could be crafted.

There was an even greater gap between the vibratory levels of the mental and emotional bodies, therefore the same procedure had to be followed, and a second interface inserted. As for attaching these bodies to the physical body, that was really a massive task, and had to be done in two separate stages. One was to create another interface, following the techniques which had been previously used for the others. However, this interface was to be far more complicated than the others, as it had to be an exact replica of the foetus to which it was to connect. So first he had to find a foetus.

The instructions said "Choose a foetus – an unborn baby growing in its mother's womb." Well, that bit at least was easy: there were hundreds of millions of women on Earth who were pregnant at that time, so Numan chose a foetus which looked strong and healthy. Now he had to create the interface for it, and that had to be an exact spiritual replica of the foetus. So he did that as well, and then he came onto the really difficult part.

He had to connect all the nerves, muscles, organs, glands and fibres in the interface with their counterparts in the physical body – and that took a long time, in fact, all of the three months which had been allocated for the task. However, the task was eventually finished, just in time.

So finally Numan was born as a human being. He was a big, strong baby, and he revelled in all the new experiences which he was having. He kicked his legs, waved his arms, wriggled his body and exercised his vocal chords. He soon found out that whenever he wanted anything he had only to shout and his doting parents would run to provide his needs – and he never got out of that habit. Most children go through the "terrible twos" period, when they find out that their own wants must sometimes be balanced with the wants of others, but Numan was never disciplined by his parents, and never learnt. When he was growing up as a child, if he wanted another child's toy, he took it, and if the child objected he just knocked him down.

The trend continued when he went to school. A big strong boy, he soon became the school bully, and this continued when he went to senior school. He found out that he could use others to do his bidding, and other weaker boys were drawn into his circle and became his "gang". He realised that he could use others to make money for himself, and started a "business", which he continued on leaving school, and – because of his ruthless methods, exploiting his workforce shamefully – he became very prosperous. He got married, and terrorised his wife, and when they had children, abused them. His whole life was a continuous story of selfishness and greed.

However, what he did not realise was that every time that he deliberately hurt anyone, the thought which preceded the action drew in negative energy from a lower dimension, which coated his mental and emotional bodies, so that by the time the physical body died, they were effectively glued together.

Well, he did eventually die, and – as per his instruction manual – his physical body separated from his subtle bodies, and he moved into the fourth dimension. However, now something went wrong: the instruction manual said that the emotional and mental bodies and their respective interfaces would fall away, and he would be able to walk through the portal into the fifth dimension, but that didn't happen. The two bodies remained locked together, and when he tried to walk towards the portal he found himself being pushed away. After several attempts, he looked round and saw someone who looked like an official. (You can always recognise an official – someone who *seems* to know what is going on.) The official told him that as his two bodies were glued together by negative energy, he couldn't go any further; and the only thing that he could do was go back to the third dimension, where the energy had been accumulated, and get rid of it.

He wasn't too unhappy about that: after all, he had thoroughly enjoyed his time in the third dimension, doing whatever gave him pleasure, so he returned and went through the whole process again. However, what he hadn't been told was that the act of going back would wipe out his memory of having been in the fourth dimension, and of what he had been told. So he repeated his experiences, harming many other people and in doing so accumulated a lot more negative energy.

This began what Buddhists call "the Wheel of Rebirth", when he had to return to the Earth over and over again to live successive lives. However, things were changing, imperceptibly: he noticed that when it came to choosing a foetus in which to be born, his choices became progressively limited. To understand the reason for this, it might be useful to think of a thunderstorm: when a storm is brewing, the physical negative ions in the clouds build up, and the positive ions on the earth also build up, until the tension between them is so great that it has to be neutralised – and a lightning strike joins the clouds and the earth and defuses the situation.

So eventually he was forced to choose a foetus which was weak and sickly, which eventually became a small child, prone to many illnesses. His parents were over-strict, almost abusively so. As he was growing up, he was the one who lost his toys to other, bigger boys, and he was the one who was bullied at school. Later in life he was exploited at work, married an abusive wife and was tormented by his own children. In fact, he led a dreadful life, and was happy when it finally ended.

When he got into the fourth dimension, the official (who by now had become an old friend,) came up to him and said, "I see that you have begun to get rid of some of your negative energy. Well done. Of course, there is a lot more to do, but at least you have made a good start." Then off he went, back into the third dimension again.

Now began a series of lives in which he was getting rid of more and more of the negativity which had built up over many incarnations, and much of the rest of his story is about his gradual realisation of what life was all about. He still hurt others, of course, but he was starting to realise why some of the harmful things which were happening to him occurred. In one life he did something to harm someone – perhaps he stole something which was dear to them – and then later in the same life he had something which he cherished deeply stolen from him in turn; and this made him wonder whether there was any connection between the two events.

In another life, he was enticed into going into a church – the denomination doesn't matter – in which there was an address on the subject of "Divine Retribution", and this made him think even more deeply, and decide to avoid hurting anyone else if it could be avoided. It made him consciously try to be more helpful to others, and in doing so he found that life was becoming more enjoyable. Because Karma works for all conditions, positive and negative, if you deliberately do something to help someone else, you in turn will be helped on a future occasion: "What goes round comes round."

So we come to the end of Numan's journey. At the end of this last life, the physical body and its interface slipped away but now, as he entered the fourth dimension, the emotional body and its interfaces also separated. However, strangely – and contrary to what it said in the manual – the mental body did not separate. He asked his friend the official why that was, and he was told that for so many lives his mental body had worked in close attunement with the spiritual body: this had been so close, in fact, that they were now welded together by positive energy, and had become a permanent entity – a soul – and this perfected soul could now progress back through the higher dimensions until it reached its true spiritual home in the tenth dimension.

So this time when he walked towards the portal, it swung open wide even before he reached it, and he walked through, a perfected soul, into the fifth dimension, at last on his way home..

Chapter Twenty-Five:
The Christmas Message
Proforma

'Beloved child,

I am asked by my instrument to give you a few words on which you can meditate at this time in your life.

Christmas is a time of joy, when most people feel the expression, on a spiritual level, of the original Love which was manifest in the birth of that small baby in a manger some two thousand years ago. At this time all try to express their love to others by the giving of presents and by gathering together socially; they usually celebrate also by treating themselves to luxuries which they would not normally be able – or willing – to indulge in at other times of the year.

From the spiritual point of view this is also the time when those who have made their transition to this side of life draw near to those whom they have left behind in your world: the vibrant energy of Love which pervades everything at this time acts like a magnet to attract them to be with their loved ones once more. Indeed, they are never more than a thought away, as in this dimension original thought and subsequent action are instantaneous, so all that is needed by them is the thought of being with you, and they are there instantly.

One thing which is not yet clearly understood by human beings is that everything in Creation is made up of the same "material" – and this "material" can best be described in your terms as "Love". This was the original force which produced the act of Creation itself, and it is still the most potent force in the

Universe. Love can be expressed in many different ways, and if you meditate on the word itself you will be amazed at the many manifestations of it in daily life. But the most amazing thing of all is that all such manifestations are part of the same basic energy: by performing an act of Love in one form, you are in effect showing it in all of its forms. By tending a sick animal or an ailing plant, by comforting a sick child or helping an aged person to cross the road, you are expressing Love in just as active a way as if you were consoling a bereaved person or even locked in the most intimate physical embrace with your soul mate.

When you realise that the love which you felt for your beloved father while he was still on the earth plane still exists - you did not stop loving him once he was no longer in the physical body, did you? - the spiritual communion between you still carries on, although the physical expression of it is no longer possible, then it could help you to start to enter into a new and wonderful phase of your life. Your father finished the tasks – and learnt the lessons – for which he originally came into this incarnation, and so he was *allowed* to return "home". But that does not mean that his association with you has ceased: far from it. It means that he is now able to work with you in ways which were not possible during his earthly life, helping, inspiring, supporting and suggesting new things which you can do *together* – so that you no longer work as *two separate* individuals, but you can work as *one*. When you rise from your bed each morning, send out a silent thought to ask him what you are going to do together during the day, and tell him of your own current intentions. You may find that thoughts come into your head which will modify your programme. Then, whatever you are doing, from time to time talk to him and include him in what is happening, just as you might once have done while he was still by your side. Finally, at the end of the day, send out your thoughts once more thanking him for being with you and helping you, and expressing your love in whatever way you wish – and feel the Love which he is able to send to you.

Now let us put this into a practical perspective: as I have said above, each act of Love that you do, however small and apparently insignificant, is an act which adds to – and is

The Christmas Message Pro-forma

sanctified by – the absolute eternal Love. Therefore, whatever you do to help others in any way (not forgetting the plant and animal kingdoms) do it out of your love for your beloved father. Dedicate it to him, and feel the Love which he expresses in return. This will mean that your life will take on a completely new meaning, as every little action will have the potential of showing your love for your father and of binding you together far more closely than you were ever bound during his physical life. (This may seem impossible to you at the moment, but once you have experienced it you will realise that it is true.)

Let me finally add a few words which have an even deeper meaning: as you know, it is a devastating experience to have to sit and watch a loved one suffering, whether that suffering is mental, emotional or physical, and to know that you are powerless to do anything to help him or her. But have you considered that that is what your beloved father, on this side of life, is experiencing when he watches you grieving? He *knows* that there is no need for continued grief, although he realises that sorrow and the pouring out of tears are an essential part of the healing process for a time after bereavement. So it will be of great benefit to him when his loved ones still on the Earth plane finally accept that he still exists, and get on with their lives. Moreover, he exists in a state which is infinitely more desirable than the one in which he was while in his earthly life. Remember that no-one who is able to communicate through a medium ever says that they would like to be back in their earthly life – because they wouldn't.

I hope that these few reflections may provide help and comfort to you at what is still a difficult time of your year.'

Chapter Twenty-Six:
Christmas Message Tailoring Instructions

Using the Christmas letter for "father" as a pro-forma, you can create separate versions for any other relative or friend, and even insert the names of people, as appropriate. This is how you do it:

Scan the pro-forma into the computer. Make a couple of copies, e.g. "proforma1", "proforma2", etc., just in case the first one gets corrupted.

Now let us imagine that you want to create a letter for "husband".

Read in the pro-forma, and immediately save as "husband". This will ensure that the original pro-forma is not overwritten.

The pro-forma is made out for a father, and so every time that the word "father" is mentioned it will have to be changed for "husband". In the "Replace" feature in Word, replace the word "father" with the word "husband". Print off the final result and see if it reads correctly; (it is far easier to read a hard copy than it is to read a computer screen.) If it is correct "save" it.

That is all you ever have to do as far as men are concerned, and you can create files for "son", "grandfather" and "brother" – or any other male relative or friend – very quickly, by doing the same exercise and replacing "father" with the new relationship.

You now have to create a file for women, and this is more complicated. First read in the pro-forma and save as "mother". In the "Replace" feature, replace the word "father" with the word "mother". Now go through the document and change every "he", "him" or "his" to "she" or "her" as appropriate. Print off the final result and see if it reads correctly. If it is correct, save it. Now repeat the process for other female relatives.

Finally, if you want to create a personalised letter for a named individual, if a male, read in the "father" file, if a female, read in the "mother" file. Now use the "Replace" feature to insert the name of the person where appropriate. Print the file off and read through to check it: you may find it needs minor adjustments where you have made your alterations.

Index

Index

www.ingramcontent.com/pod-product-compliance
Lightning Source LLC
La Vergne TN
LVHW052024080426
835513LV00018B/2141